Helen Hope

# Star babies
## astrology for babies
### and their parents

CITADEL PRESS
Kensington Publishing Corp.
www.kensingtonbooks.com

CITADEL PRESS BOOKS are published by

Kensington Publishing Corp.
850 Third Avenue
New York, NY 10022

First published in Australia in 2003 by HarperCollinsPublishers Pty Limited.
Published by arrangement with HarperCollins Publishers Pty Limited

All Kensington titles, imprints, and distributed lines are available at special quantity discounts for bulk purchases for sales promotions, premiums, fund-raising, educational, or institutional use. Special book excerpts or customized printings can also be created to fit specific needs. For details, write or phone the office of the Kensington special sales manager: Kensington Publishing Corp., 850 Third Avenue, New York, NY 10022, attn: Special Sales Department; phone 1-800-221-2647.

CITADEL PRESS and the Citadel logo are Reg. U.S. Pat. & TM Off.

First printing: January 2005

10   9   8   7   6   5   4   3   2   1

Printed in the United States of America

Cataloging data may be obtained from the Library of Congress.

ISBN 0 8065-2673-4

To all the babies yet to be,
and all the babies that ever were

# Contents

## STAR BABIES

## STAR PARENTS

# Star babies

The whole human race is seen in every baby's face.

*Anon.*

# Aries
# baby

21 March – 20 April

ARCHANGEL: Samael, The angel of righteousness

BIRTHSTONE: Ruby

METAL: iron

COLOR: Scarlet

HERB: Garlic

FLOWER: Gladiolus

TREE: Traditional — Chestnut

COUNTRIES: England, Denmark

CITIES: Florence, Marseilles

AGAINST THE CAPITOL I MET A LION, WHO GLARED UPON ME, AND WENT SURLY BY WITHOUT ANNOYING ME. — Shakespeare, *Julius Caesar*

If you desire a charismatic, dynamic baby, one that's born with a healthy sense of self, then you need look no further than this first Sign of the Zodiac.

"First" describes the nucleus of the Arien character traits rather aptly. Ariens are assigned to Mars, the warrior planet, and can be feisty and fiery as well as courageous and noble. Mars not only endows baby Aries with great reserves of energy, but also the ability for single-minded focus that results in the attainment of goals impossible without this character quality. Unfortunately, this has led to Ariens being branded as "me-first" people. This is not true. We all have the capacity for selfishness and it's only seen in the Aries child who has not been taught to share and consider others. It is not an inborn state of being.

However, with the Arien passion for life and impatience to get going, it is quite possible that baby Aries will arrive a little before the due date, and do so rapidly, sparing Mother a protracted labor.

The Arien star baby can also be impatient to get its tiny (which it won't be for long — this star child's lust for life packs robust body weight on) physical form into working action. This baby wants to explore the new world, and do so NOW! Thus, baby Aries can become mobile quickly, sometimes even dispensing with crawling, and going direct to walking as early as nine or ten months!

But this desire to get moving can result in frustrated crying in early babyhood days. If so, an interesting and brightly colored feature hung above the bassinet will capture the infant's interest. You can use your imagination here. Another good way to calm baby Aries is, after a little loving cuddle, to put baby on a blanket and gently work those little limbs. An Aries star baby loves feeling the muscles in its tiny legs and arms being flexed, and the blood circulating around its body. Much nicer than being concentrated in a red and yowling face!

Actually, that brings up another point. When baby does achieve independent mobility, and perhaps even before, always keep a watchful eye. This star baby is renowned for its impulsive activities resulting in a bump on the head or a scratch on the face. Fear is something baby Aries does not have much of, and will rush in where angels fear to tread. Note "rush." The Aries baby is one you cannot turn your back on for a moment. Faster than the speed of light, this star baby will head for the closest trouble spot around. And do not make the mistake of thinking you've checked and there are none. There always is, and baby Aries in motion will always find them.

However, this is all part of baby Aries' pioneering, enthusiastic nature: the inner drive that can take your star baby to success in adulthood. Aries will often make bags of money on the way and provide for parents, even though this child may be the first to leave home!

Your Aries child is likely to excel on the sports field as well. These star children do not lack in intelligence, but they do lack patience when being taught in boring and repetitive ways. Not that you'll want to change anything. Your first look into your little bundle of joy's eyes will reveal an independent character peering out. You will be instantly captivated and conquered, and know you have a little winner in your charge, whose best causes and qualities are your delight and duty to champion.

**TO SUMMARIZE:** Full of energy, the Aries baby simply can't wait to get going — and can be somewhat demanding until doing so! But once mobile and busy on projects, tears and tantrums cease. In the meantime, big red toys and things that make interesting noises will keep this star baby happily involved. Success awaits these little Mars people.

**MOST IMPORTANT LESSONS:** Patience and sharing.

**SUITABLE VOCATIONS:** Engineering, military, sports, medicine, show business entrepreneur.

## WELL-PARENTED ARIENS

Elle Macpherson ✳ Leonardo da Vinci ✳ St. Theresa of Avila ✳ Sir Robert Helpmann ✳ Jennifer Capriati ✳ General William Booth (founded Salvation Army) ✳ Doris Day ✳ Sir Alec Guinness

## NOT SO WELL-PARENTED ARIENS

Vincent van Gogh ✳ Bette Davis ✳ Casanova ✳ Mary Pickford ✳ Lucrezia Borgia ✳ Harry Houdini ✳ Goya ✳ Prince Bismarck

# Taurus
## baby

21 April – 20 May

ARCHANGEL: Haneil, The angel of love

BIRTHSTONE: Emerald

METAL: Copper

COLOR: Verdant green

HERB: Cloves

FLOWER: Rose

TREE: Traditional — Walnut

COUNTRIES: ireland, Switzerland

CITIES: Dublin, ST Louis

BUT, STILL, SWEET LOVE IS FOOD FOR FORTUNE'S TOOTH.
— Shakespeare, *Troilus and Cressida*

Thinking about a cuddly, patient, loving little soul to parent? Well, baby Taurus could be exactly the star baby destined for you.

Beautiful Venus, planet of peace and prosperity, tends to infant Taureans in her Earth Empress form. As well as lending star baby Taurus a little luck (Taureans are often born with a "silver spoon in their mouths," as the old saying goes, or are delivered as the youngest and therefore doted on by now-skilled parents), Venus also endows a beauty that goes beyond the mere physical into an aura of magnetic attraction coupled with grace of spirit. Is it any wonder that people are drawn to baby talk and goo to tiny Taureans, who will certainly goo and gurgle back.

But don't think that this star baby is emotionally superficial and wanton. Tiny Taurus loves everybody, as in the ideal world that's how it is. (Remember, baby Taurus has just left heaven, where love is the paramount emotion, and imbues all.) However, when it comes to Mama and Papa, it's hard to match this star baby's parental devotion. You will see your little Taurean's face light up when you come into view bending over the crib, and a look of abject disappointment in your baby's eyes if you then try to withdraw without even picking them up for a cuddle! Your little Taurean's first word might even be

"Mine!" uttered with their plump little arms clasped around your neck. When your star baby becomes an adult you'll experience their generosity of spirit (Venus is also a "money" planet and many Taureans acquire generous amounts of wealth too!), which manifests in wonderful and devotedly traditional ways of honoring and caring for parents.

This star baby is usually quite passionate about food as well. It is great not having a troublesome feeder as a baby, but do watch out for overeating, especially when tiny Taurus becomes able to totter about and out of your eye range. Even when a baby, best to have a judicious feeding schedule. Generous amounts, sure. But not too much. If baby Taurus is too greedy, upset tummies and colic result. Not much fun for anyone, least of all for this usually placid star child.

The Taurus baby then bellows, revealing another side to the dulcet voice power bestowed by Venus. As this Sign's stamina is symbolized by the bull, the Taurus baby can keep it up for some time!

Do not allow doting grandparents, aunts, uncles or whoever to constantly proffer chocolates, lollipops and such to toddler Taurus either. Rather, foster and refine the renowned Taurean sweet tooth through fruits and other natural goodies; such as honey for sweetening, and carob for treats. Your teenage Taurus will thank you for keeping them slim, taut and terrific (and healthy!).

And that raises another issue. If not guided in other directions, some Taureans can become couch potatoes. Vital staying power simply becomes inertia. So, begin good habits early, both dietary and otherwise. Encourage mobility as a baby and ensure plenty of outdoor activities and at least one dedicated sport as a youngster.

As already alluded to, the Taurean voice is usually a gifted one. Many singers, classical to hip-hop, are born under the Taurus star. Musicality and rhythm resonate in this Sign and your star child could be highly talented. Watch them with keyboards or a set of drums at age two or before!

All babies will be upset at times, but with Taureans it can be for inscrutable reasons. Their loving natures are deep and complex; it might be that you paid too much attention to the cat! As Taurean babies thrive on lullabies, being tenderly held and sung to is a guaranteed way to calm this star infant and bring reassurance. Even better when you walk around the garden as well, showing your Taurean little one the lovely green trees and pretty flowers out there. After all, baby Taurus has a very special connection to Mother Nature, and her beauty works magic in the development of your star child's unique gifts. Even more precious is the stable and loving environment you provide in which your divine little treasure from heaven can blossom and bloom.

TO SUMMARIZE: Small Taureans can be complex bundles of mystery. The key is simple; lots of cuddles and affection. This brings cozy feelings of security and being wanted, encouraging development of the great artistic and practical gifts they are born with. Little Taureans may slowly, but will surely, find their path to success — just remember to introduce changes thoughtfully and curb a tendency to overeat.

**MOST IMPORTANT LESSONS:** Fruitful activity and confident self-expression.

**SUITABLE VOCATIONS:** Singing, finance, horticulture, sculptor, fashion, peacemaker, ambassador.

### WELL-PARENTED TAUREANS
Queen Elizabeth II * Benjamin Spock * Dame Nellie Melba * Ella Fitzgerald * William Shakespeare * Margot Fonteyn * Harry S. Truman

### NOT SO WELL-PARENTED TAUREANS
Oliver Cromwell * Maximilien Robespierre * Adolf Hitler * Salvador Dali * Sigmund Freud * Liberace * Niccolò Machiavelli

Gemini
baby

21 May – 21 June

ARCHANGEL: Raphael, angel of progress

BIRTHSTONE: Aquamarine

METAL: Quicksilver

COLOR: Crystal blue

HERB: Parsley

FLOWER: Lily of The Valley

TREE: Traditional — Elder

COUNTRIES: United States, Lower Egypt

CITIES: London, Melbourne

BE CALM, GOOD WIND, BLOW NOT A WORD AWAY TILL I HAVE FOUND EACH LETTER IN THE LETTER. — Shakespeare, *Two Gentlemen of Verona*

**A**re you taken by the thought of having a charming, versatile and bewitching little bundle of joy in your charge? Then magical, mercurial star baby Gemini might be the answer to your prayer.

However, you will have to parent this tiny package of paradoxes highly skilfully and very sensitively. Fundamental paradox number one is that this star infant needs quality sleep, and lots of it, but can be woken by the sound of a pin dropping. Another paradox is that baby Gemini can be so happy, vivaciously dazzling all and sundry, including the dog, that sleep is the last thing they desire to succumb to. And, although completely exhausted, they will fight it with their complete repertoire of snooze prevention tactics — from enthralling you with the essence of cute pervading baby's aura and scintillating eyes, to becoming so overstimulated that all they can do is cry.

But with just a little knowledge of what makes baby Gemini tick, the latter sorry state of affairs need never occur. Clever Mercury watches over Geminians. Masterful Mercury, consummate communicator and synchronistic connector (not for nothing is it said, "The art of magic is the art of timing"), has sovereignty over the human nervous system, as well as lungs, arms and hands. This results in your little Gemini being finely and highly tuned consciously, and alert to movement and sound in the environment. Just having this understanding enables you to ensure baby's nursery is in a quiet, but well-aired (fresh, clean air is another "must" for this star baby's well-being) part of the house, and to also ensure that your Gemini infant is not overexcited prior to nap time. By setting good sleeping patterns early, you give your star child the context in which its dynamic nature can thrive, and those diverse Geminian gifts flourish. And you enjoy the blessing of having the ingenious infant of the Zodiac, rather than the insomniac version.

So, quiet time before bed time and ensuring a peaceful slumber space are essential to baby Gemini's optimum development. And don't be hoodwinked by your star baby's attempts to outwit you (remember, this is a very smart baby!) in delaying bed time.

A well nurtured, well slept little Gemini is joy in human form. Their dear little, usually uniquely attractive, faces, with bright inquisitive eyes and exquisite little smiles, spark chain reactions of wonder and happiness in whoever beholds them — not just you, the lucky parents. A quintessential vignette of the power of this star baby's "cute" is seen in a 1934 photograph of infant Joan Collins with a sign "Please do not kiss" hung on the handle of her carriage. Her mother had become tired of the legions of strangers being drawn, as moths to the flame, to little Gemini Joan's fledgling charisma.

Establishing good communication with your Gemini child early is also another important key to development. Even when this baby is still in the womb, chats and little conversations stimulate and cement an even closer and more precious child–parent relationship. Talking gently with your newborn Gemini also helps them feel more at home on planet Earth, after the glory of heaven. Look deeply into those little eyes too — you will see understanding in there.

As your star baby grows, don't forget to factor in reading at least one story a day. Gemini's imagination, creativity and inner evolutionary faculties are sparked by the sounds of words. When baby is upset, tenderly picking baby up, speaking in gentle, but coherent tones, and lightly walking around, at the same time pointing out little features of interest, like a bird flying, a bright flower and so on, soon brings calm, and baby Gemini quickly unwinds from being overwrought.

Bright baby disco-balls, miniature angels or stars hung over the crib can fascinate this little one for hours. Just make sure the light emitted is safe, and take them down periodically so that interest is renewed when hung again. You could also hang letters and numbers where baby can see them. But don't push your star child's intellectual development. As with a flower, if given the right climate, it will just unfold. Some Gemini children spontaneously read at four years. Suddenly the words make sense. The same with numbers. At age four and a bit, Gemini has worked out how to count to one hundred. One of this star infant's most beloved toys can be the old fashioned rag story book and, in fact, all Gemini children should have at least one.

By now you will have gathered that you have a sensitive, but astute and highly aware being in your star child. So do not be surprised if your baby starts vocalizing early, and you hear definite words by six months. And don't be surprised if it is, "Why?"

**TO SUMMARIZE:** This tiny charmer of the Zodiac has the ability to wind everyone around its little finger. These outgoing, bright, curious and often precocious little stars have special destinies to fulfil. Gemini baby's sensitive nerves can easily be jangled, and crying often results; but soft talking, walking and gentle rocking brings calm. Their nimble minds and quick talking will win them many prizes.

**MOST IMPORTANT LESSONS:** Focus and follow through.

**SUITABLE VOCATIONS:** Journalism, teaching, media industry, writing, actor, facilitator, trouble shooter.

## WELL-PARENTED GEMINIANS
Sir Laurence Olivier ✳ John F. Kennedy ✳ Socrates ✳ Queen Victoria ✳ Sir Paul McCartney ✳ Richard Wagner ✳ Nicole Kidman ✳ Frank Lloyd Wright

## NOT SO WELL-PARENTED GEMINIANS
Dr Joseph Guillotin ✳ Isadora Duncan ✳ Jean Cocteau ✳ Marquis de Sade ✳ Marilyn Monroe ✳ Errol Flynn ✳ Jean-Paul Sartre ✳ Beau Brummell

# Cancer
## baby

22 June – 23 July

ARCHANGEL: Gabriel, angel of aspirations and dreams

BIRTHSTONE: Pearl

METAL: Silver

COLOR: White

HERB: Tarragon

FLOWER: Gardenia

TREE: Traditional — Willow

COUNTRIES: Scotland, Holland

CITIES: New York, Tokyo

GO TO YOUR BOSOM; KNOCK THERE AND ASK YOUR HEART WHAT IT
DOTH KNOW. — Shakespeare, *Measure for Measure*

I f you want a child who is sympathetic yet industrious, sensitive yet sociable and, above all, highly lovable, a Cancerian babe is your kinder-kismet.

The nurturing Moon is the heavenly body that guides the Cancerian star. The influence of the Moon's rays upon germinating seeds and the ocean's tides is observable fact and indicates the depth of emotion in this little star of the Zodiac. Since antiquity the Moon has been associated with home and hearth, and this points to the great love of family your tiny Cancerian is born with. Parents are at the top of the tree: Mother, in particular, has great influence on her Cancerian child, so best to ensure this always works to the good. The whole kit and kaboodle of relatives, including long-gone ancestors (many grown-up Cancerians feel driven to research family lineage), are also intrinsic to little Cancer's reality reference points.

These star children are highly receptive, even when tiny babies (perhaps even more so then!), so always make sure that the environment and vibrations they are subject to are harmonious and loving. You do not want lasting wrong impressions distorting your Cancerian's outlook. Nor do you want them brooding over unnecessary hurts inflicted in youth, in adulthood.

A secure, well-loved and well-parented Cancerian child will grow into one of the most effective and influential adults on the planet. Their great love of family extends to the human family, and there's a desire to better the lot of all. However, the adult Cancerian will always put their parents first and lovingly fulfill their filial duties — usually going way beyond the point of call. Cancerians can be shrewd financially, and you can be sure the dollars will be found to fund any matter important to parents' well-being. Little investments growing into big assets, as well as money hidden away for that rainy day, are all part of Cancer's portfolio.

Cancer star babies are usually enthusiastic about their nutrition and will suckle well. Breast-feeding is wonderful for all babies and is particularly good for this infant. When your little Moon child's appetite is lackluster, the reasons are probably emotionally based. They like their sleep and if fretfulness breaks a formerly good pattern, then emotional upset is the likely culprit. Loads of unconditional love, expressed as affectionate and understanding cuddles, will help your star baby find a happy equilibrium again.

The emotions and digestive system influence each other strongly in the Cancerian make-up. An unhappy baby will cry, fret and become colicky; whereas a content infant will be a chubby, confident and cuddly little charmer. In those rare instances where baby Cancer is crying uncontrollably, it is time for a bath. Yes, that's right, get out all the paraphernalia and pamper baby with warm, soapy, scented tubbing. Let water run in rivulets over your little one's tummy, move them gently around in the bath and see those eyes quieten into joy as baby experiences the fun of water and bath time. A gentle massage with perfumed baby oil afterwards also works miracles.

The Cancerian star child can be one of the most rewarding to parent. As a baby, Cancer radiates archetypal appeal (somewhat similar to the effect that pictures of cherubs have), melting even the crustiest of hearts and making you a very proud parent. As a youngster your star child will listen to you, as well as take their cues from you. As adults, no matter how successful they become, your Cancerian will never lose sight of who they owe it all to — and that's Mom and Dad. Mind you, this is the Cancerian who has been raised by parents with an awareness of their star child's great sensitivity, and have not allowed others to be cruel to their progeny but have worked to promote the reverse. Parents who have fostered self-confidence and positive experiences for their child, as well as allowing the child its funny little ways, knowing that Cancer's moods can fluctuate like the Moon. Suffice it to say, the misunderstood Cancerian can be the most miserable child on Earth.

But this will never happen in your family. From the moment you hold your newborn, and feel like your precious little charge is somehow hugging you back, you know destiny has brought you together for very special purposes. You will strive always to protect your star baby's sensitive vulnerability, because you also know that will become the child's greatest strength. Your star baby will love comfy soft toys and joyful baths, and will grow into solid food quite early, letting you get more sleep at night. And the first word will be "Mama" or "Dada" — you can bank on it.

**TO SUMMARIZE:** Cancer babies are extremely impressionable. All the new sensations they experience have a great impact and are indelibly etched into their memories, so make them good ones. Their expressive little faces will let you know! The right stimulation banishes boredom and builds success. They are born romantics, and they can make their dreams become reality.

**MOST IMPORTANT LESSONS:** Emotional balance and self-belief.

**SUITABLE VOCATIONS:** Hospitality, novelist, media personality or anchorperson, composer, nursing.

## WELL-PARENTED CANCERIANS
Tom Hanks * Princess Diana * Gustav Mahler * Dr. Barnardo * Sir Edmund Hillary * Ringo Starr * Louis Armstrong * Julius Caesar

## NOT SO WELL-PARENTED CANCERIANS
Franz Kafka * Ernest Hemingway * Samuel Colt * George Orwell * Modigliani * Barbara Cartland * George Sand * Iris Murdoch

# Leo baby

24 July – 23 August

ARCHANGEL: Michael, angel of light

BIRTHSTONE: Diamond

METAL: Gold

COLOR: Saffron yellow

HERB: Dandelion

FLOWER: Sunflower

TREE: Traditional — Palm

COUNTRIES: France, Sicily

CITIES: Rome, Los Angeles

I AM AS CONSTANT AS THE NORTHERN STAR, OF WHOSE TRUE-FIXED AND RESTING QUALITY THERE IS NO FELLOW IN THE FIRMAMENT. — Shakespeare, *Julius Caesar*

**W**ould you like an affectionate, loyal child, whose regal tilt of the head commands the attention of everyone in the room? Then little Leo is obviously fated for you.

But get ready for a strong, self-willed child. One who is quite ready to trot out the dramatics to get its own way or if feeling not enough attention is being accorded to its royal self. You need to establish the ground rules early. Do not be intimidated into kowtowing to your star child's demands, especially when you know it's against baby's best interests. But do ensure your star infant understands that oodles of unconditional love surround it at all times. You will be rewarded by seeing little Leo's dramatic abilities become wonderfully productive and entertaining, rather than simply demanding.

Leo baby's amazing strength (many can hold their heads high soon after birth) and vitality has much to do with the Sun's association with Leo. In ancient times, the Sign of Leo was seen as the domicile of the Sun. All Leos were blessed by the rays of the Sun. The life-giving Sun is the powerhouse of our solar system. It stays fixed, while everything revolves around it. (That latter sentence should give you more clues as to why it is not a good idea to let your infant Leo learn tyranny as a behavioral technique, but also why it is very important your baby knows it is always held in high and loving regard.) In times when childbirth was more perilous, a Leo child was perceived as better equipped for survival, as the life force itself was accompanying them on their earthly journey.

It comes as no surprise that Leo is the Sign primarily associated with royalty and ruling. Indeed, many contemporary royals have the Sun or Leo strongly situated in their astrological makeup. Riches too are abundant in this Sign. A certain "Midas" touch, coupled with the Leonine strong force of will, means if they are not born into lots of moolah, they will make a tidy sum on their way.

That is, if you have parented in first-class style and your wonderful star child's gifts are in excellent working order. You don't want a lazy lion, expecting others to provide plus wait on them hand and foot, one who will bite off heads if there's any complaint! No. You want the sunny-natured, charismatic and successful Leonine qualities fully developed. There may be some battles of wills along the way, but your star child will be all the better for it. It is vitally important that the Leo child can look up to and respect Mater and Pater.

This star of the Zodiac likes to be as proud of their parents as their parents are of them. The pride of lions is legendary. It's no coincidence that a family of lions is referred to as a "pride." The pride dynamic in good working order (not muted or distorted via dysfunctional family syndrome) enables the nobility and majesty inherent in your Leo child's nature to flourish. These are not ego qualities so much as character qualities. The difference being that the former are assumed and irritating, whereas the latter simply shine through, uplifting others and prompting them to reach for their best.

The Leo Zodiac star is famed for its leadership powers (whether as head of state or a safari team), its ability to oversee operations that require inspiration, and being able to cleverly relate everyone involved to the bigger picture (roles such as stage manager, film director, motivational speaker). The Leonine ability to help lesser stars shine more brightly can be phenomenal.

A practical way to guide your warm-hearted and sometimes hot-headed little Leo towards highly successful development of their innate gifts is to always treat your little one with respect, and make this a two-way street by expecting the same back. Ensure your little Leo feels a part of everything. (At a family barbecue, for example, infant Leo would enjoy being handed around and oohed and aahed over — even if still in swaddling clothes!) Encourage your Leonine child's self-expression by supplying a versatile dress-up box and be unfailingly enthusiastic about their productions. Sport, dance and music lessons also help foster your Leonine's star qualities.

Your journey together begins with the spark of great love (and pride!) your newborn brings, is accompanied by the joy of your Leo infant's unfolding (plus an increasing swag of rewards and prizes as the years go on!) and is blessed by the undying love forged between you as baby Leo hits adult success and stardom. And, as sure as the sunrise tomorrow, your star child will make sure that you never want for anything.

**TO SUMMARIZE:** Leo babies are charming, funny and playful, but sometimes only as long as they get their own way! When these intransigent little Leos don't, the ensuing roar can be heard by the deafest of neighbors. Tiny lions can tend to dominate the household, but this is compensated by their essentially sunny natures. A little guidance will help them reach the top as adults.

**MOST IMPORTANT LESSONS:** Gratitude and adaptability.

**SUITABLE VOCATIONS:** Thespian, director, judge, head of any business enterprise, entertainment industry, prize athlete, chef.

## WELL-PARENTED LEOS
Queen Mother * Alexander the Great * Jacqueline Kennedy Onassis * Cecil B. DeMille * Princess Margaret * Carl G. Jung * Magic Johnson * Princess Anne * Lucille Ball

## NOT SO WELL-PARENTED LEOS
George Bernard Shaw * Napoleon Bonaparte * Fidel Castro * Andy Warhol * Mae West * Emily Brontë * Emperor Claudius * Benito Mussolini

# Virgo baby

## 24 August – 23 September

ARCHANGEL: Adonai, angel of redemption

BIRTHSTONE: Sapphire

METAL: Titanium

COLOR: Indigo

HERB: Fennel

FLOWER: Jasmine

TREE: Traditional — Hazel

COUNTRIES: New Zealand, Greece

CITIES: Paris, Jerusalem

AND THIS OUR LIFE, EXEMPT FROM PUBLIC HAUNT, FINDS TONGUES IN TREES, BOOKS IN THE RUNNING BROOKS, SERMONS IN THE STONES, AND GOOD IN EVERYTHING. — Shakespeare, *As You Like It*

I f you yearn for an appealing, considerate and reliable child, baby Virgo can more than fit those aspirations.

However, you need to be aware that you have a highly sensitive soul to parent. And this is from day one. There is an enigmatic quality to Virgo, which can work to mask their true needs and feelings. The more this happens, the more the Virgo star child's considerable potential is buried. So cradle your newborn little Virgo in your arms straightaway and ensure baby feels all your love and blessed welcome. There will come a moment when you deeply "know" that little baby Virgo now believes that you truly love them and want them in your life forever. This step is a highly important one in your child–parent relationship. Now you will be able to build on a rock-solid bond, because your Virgo child will not have a quivering sense of self-worth at the center of their being. This inner, mostly unconscious, self-doubt can cause many Virgoans to fall short of their potential.

Mercury, planet of intelligence and communication, is assigned to the Virgoan Zodiac star tribe. (Ancient texts say Mercury is caretaking Virgo until its true ruling planet is discovered. It is said that Vulcan or Hephaistos, as this planet is called, is hidden in the photosphere of the Sun.) Virgo is an Earth Sign, so practicality and dexterity are how Mercury expresses through Virgo. However, your little star child has a highly tuned nervous system, thanks to the governance of inquisitive and intelligent Mercury.

This combination causes little Virgo to constantly question all that is around them, while at the same time leaving baby open to undue noise and bad vibrations disturbing their world, fraying still-forming nerves. So the next crucial step is to ensure a peaceful and predictable environment around your tiny star child. This allows your baby to get on with the task of consolidating its central nervous system outside of the womb and to build on the deep and sacred trust between you.

A Virgo infant stressed by noise and other seemingly alarming occurrences (remember, baby is a recent arrival from peaceful paradise) becomes fractious and decidedly unhappy. Because Virgoan tummies react negatively to stress, baby Virgo is likely to lose interest in eating or evince other tummy problems. However, if you've been reading carefully, your precious gift from heaven will never be subjected to disorder during those vital early days and months, and this period of calm will lay a framework for future marvellous development of the loving bond between you. These star children usually have a unique contribution to make to society and civilization.

When baby is unsettled, perhaps teething, or because unfamiliar people are in the house, a walk outside among trees and in fresh air can work wonders. It helps Virgo baby inwardly center and find new strength to deal with whatever the situation is. (Quite magical little creatures, these Virgo babes, when given the opportunity!) Gentle communication and conversation from you also help your Virgo infant feel a lot better. If you look deeply into your little one's eyes, you will see a depth of comprehension surprising in one so young. (Get used to it, as the well-parented Virgo child will come forth, out of the blue, with pearls of understanding and astute assessments that can be startlingly pertinent.) Soft toys and blankets are comforting for baby Virgo as well. Often this star infant will develop an attachment to a special blanket, and, even when able to toddle, continue to lug it about.

The sight and sound of bells or windchimes gently tinkling are both soothing and stimulating for the Virgoan infant. As baby grows, little shows from you employing hand puppets and appropriate voices will delight and further stimulate your Virgo star's creativity. A pet, especially a cat or dog, is another amazing stimulus to your star child's development. Don't be surprised to see toddler Virgo lecturing said pet, complete with visual aids, caring for it tenderly with toy stethoscope around its neck, or just sitting with pet in blissful silence.

But most of all, your Virgo child will love you. They will be grateful to you for guiding them through life's sometimes treacherous waters, and appreciative of your understanding of their complex character, which sometimes baffle others. Your Virgoan child will quietly ensure that all matters concerning you — from mowing the lawn to a decent place to live — are seen to.

**TO SUMMARIZE:** Even when quite tiny, baby Virgo is alert and quick, but at the same time needs peace and tranquillity. Their seemingly contradictory nature can challenge and soothe in turn. Just give lots of love while they are developing their finely tuned natures and you will have the joy of raising a multi-talented individual.

**MOST IMPORTANT LESSONS:** Emotional expression and self-worth.

**SUITABLE VOCATIONS:** Healing arts, accountant, author, research, science, computers, informative media.

## WELL-PARENTED VIRGOANS

Richard Attenborough * Agatha Christie * Sir Donald Bradman * Count Leo Tolstoy * Sophia Loren * Confucius * Mother Theresa * Lord Ernest Rutherford * Lauren Bacall

## NOT SO WELL-PARENTED VIRGOANS

Captain William Bligh * Queen Elizabeth I * Brian Epstein * F. Scott Fitzgerald * Freddie Mercury * Greta Garbo * Cardinal Richelieu * Peter Sellers * D. H. Lawrence

# Libra baby

24 September – 23 October

ARCHANGEL: Sandalphon, angel of fruitfulness

BIRTHSTONE: Opal

METAL: Bronze

COLOR: Pink

HERB: Mint

FLOWER: Violet

TREE: Traditional — Apple

COUNTRIES: Upper Egypt, China

CITIES: Copenhagen, Vienna

HEAVEN WOULD IN LITTLE SHOW. THEREFORE HEAVEN NATURE CHARGED THAT ONE BODY SHOULD BE FILLED WITH ALL GRACES WIDE ENLARGED. — Shakespeare, *As You Like It*

If you find the thought of a diplomatic, cooperative and sociable child appealing, then little Libra could well be your dream come true.

Especially if you also want qualities such as "cute" and "charming" in the kind of quotas that bag prizes at baby shows. In fact, if this is what you are quite set on, then perhaps you should sign baby Libra up with an agent as well as that premier preschool! The legendary attractiveness and enchanting aura of the Libran Zodiac star comes from lovely Venus, in her Olympian goddess form, fulfilling her assignment to watch over all Librans. To this end she endows infant Libra with a potent charm that can disarm all obstacles, plus attract advantageous circumstances. Little Libra begins in early days, possibly before exiting the womb, to exercise these star qualities.

However, there is up and down, yin and yang, black and white, and the point of harmonic balance. Your tiny star baby, born under the Sign of the Scales, is here to actively learn that and you are there to assist them. Otherwise indecisiveness or undue influence by others could halt your Libran star from reaching full potential later on. It is hard for Librans, whether baby or adult, to remain emotionally stable if there is discord around them. So from day one ensure that peace and happiness surround your infant, accompanied by loads of cuddles and quality time with you. Then that precious point of balance is never lost, and your child will confidently stride through life finding all the special opportunities destiny has for them.

If upset for some reason, this baby responds well to pampering. (Wrapped in a cashmere shawl. Sleeping in the finest damask sheets. Being talcumed after a warm soapy bath. That kind of thing.) Gentle, beautiful music, classical or otherwise, also soothes this little soul, especially when held in your warm and loving arms. Watch what soft toys your baby responds to as well. Little Libra may quickly take a shine to some, and not like others at all. Your sensitive star baby derives comfort from loved toys, and the opposite from loathed ones. (This applies to people as well.) So it is important to be aware of this. Then baby can nestle with favorite "friends," and not be irritated by unwanted company.

Another fundamental is to ensure all fluids ingested by your Libran star baby are clean and pollutant free. Libran's tiny systems do not react well to contaminants, so examine all ingredients in prepared baby nutriments. But don't stint on the fluids as the Libran infant needs to be kept well hydrated for robust health. Be careful of encouraging sweet tooth problems (for example, refusing to eat pureed vegetables because they want dessert in babyhood, and a lifetime problem with chocolate in adulthood!) as well. Do not pander to baby's obvious delight in puddings and treats. Balance (there's that word again!) this out by cultivating your tiny Libran's taste for wholesome and savory foods.

Something else highly important to your star baby is love and companionship. The Sign of Libra is where the principle of relationships and interaction with others resides, so it is natural for your little one to want to reach out and be involved. Nothing chills this Venus ruled star tribe more than frosty vibes of unwelcomeness and exclusion. However, when receiving constructive and worthwhile attention Librans respond with their naturally warm and loving nature. This usually results in them being circled by the admiring and the smitten. And your tiny star will be no exception. So converse warmly and happily with your baby, and ensure your little Libran doesn't feel left out. Then before you know it, infant Libra will be superbly delighting all and sundry at gatherings, and you may have to assert your parental rights to have baby returned to you! But this you must do, because your star infant can get so wound up in the admiration evoked that the important point of balance (that crucial dynamic that will take them surely and irrevocably to success in adulthood) is passed and can get lost. Balancing play with rest is a fundamental area you need to format early on in your star child's routine. Remain firm, and politely say no to those relatives beseeching you to let gurgly, cuddly Libra continue to be handed around like an enchanting parcel.

Music, dance and dress-up all exercise your Libran's latent gifts. As a youngster, lessons in musical composition and other varieties of the arts nourish your star child's future, plus keep the harmonic point of balance well oiled. Libran children are quite actively intelligent. Tutoring them in mathematics, for example, can lead to astonishing breakthroughs. But to fully mobilize the Libran ambition and intellect there has to be an interest in the subject or quest. Another benefit arising from the Libran child receiving formalized training is that they learn not to put off what should be done today until tomorrow. Thus their considerable abilities to generate money and success are not rusted through inactivity. The old "*mañana*" syndrome can trap undisciplined Librans.

A contented and healthy Libran child is a beauteous sight indeed. Libra baby is endearingly cheerful and charming, looking like a little angel from heaven (which your tiny Libran star definitely is!), the light of love dances all around and beams from baby's eyes, warming everyone's hearts in a wonderful way. But most of all, yours. Because you will never forget the amazing force of love that united you at baby's birth. You see it always in their eyes, and they in yours. Your adult Libran will not only look after you, but also make you very proud of them.

TO SUMMARIZE: Libra babies often look as if they have just come down from heaven. These are the winners of baby shows and, with the right parenting, they are winners in life too. Don't encourage laziness, but they do need peace and quiet in large doses. That's because they play hard and then have to rest while they gather themselves for the next onslaught.

MOST IMPORTANT LESSONS: Decisiveness and moderation.

SUITABLE VOCATIONS: Diplomat, law, model, psychologist, beauty industry, film star, musician, counsellor.

## WELL-PARENTED LIBRANS
George Gershwin * Julie Andrews * Sir Marcus Oliphant * Brigitte Bardot * Ray Charles * Olivia Newton-John * Franz Liszt * Susan Sarandon * Guiseppe Verdi

## NOT SO WELL-PARENTED LIBRANS
Groucho Marx * Katherine Mansfield * Friedrich Wilhelm Nietzsche * Truman Capote * Leon Trotsky * John Lennon * Diana Dors * Oscar Wilde

# Scorpio baby

## 24 October – 22 November

ARCHANGEL: Azazel, angel of Transformation

BIRTHSTONE: Black pearl

METAL: Steel

COLOR: Maroon

HERB: Basil

FLOWER: Geranium

TREE: Traditional — Cypress

COUNTRIES: Norway, Morocco

CITIES: Washington, DC, Liverpool, UK

WE CALL A NETTLE BUT A NETTLE; AND THE FAULTS OF FOOLS BUT FOLLY. — Shakespeare, *Coriolanus*

If the thought of parenting a courageous, resourceful and intuitive individual grabs you, then baby Scorpio is surely meant for you.

The depth and profundity of these little souls is without measure, and it can be quite unnerving for some people to look into the Scorpio child's gaze. Not only is the power revealed in one so small somewhat disconcerting, but also the x-ray vision of the Scorpio star, which sees way beyond any kind of appearances and kitchy coo into the truth of one's being. It can unseat the more fainthearted amongst us. Not that this star baby sets out to disconcert others. That powerful and unlimited dimension is just part of the Scorpio Zodiac star's nature. This inborn commanding capacity is often accompanied by an awareness that has some tiny Scorpions shading their eyes from birth in order to not frighten or reveal too much to those unable to handle the strength of the Scorpio star's character.

However, you can, and your precious gift from heaven trusts in you for wise guidance in the ways of this world. Then when your Scorpio star hits adulthood, the amazing contribution they have to make to the revitalization and renewal of our planet and civilization will be unfurled, undamaged.

But back to babyhood. Tiny Scorpio forms habit patterns early. The Sign of Scorpio is one of the most powerful in the Zodiac. There is a very strong will and determination to accomplish whatever is required to be achieved. Obviously, it is highly important that your little Scorpio only be subject to positive and loving vibrations very early on. First impressions impact strongly on this Zodiac star, and have much to do with shaping their basic mode of response. A negative, non-loving and miserable environment can twist the Scorpio soul into a bitter, dangerous and mean machine indeed. Whereas a well-loved and well brought up Scorpio is capable of saving the world.

To truly understand the mystery, majesty and magic of Scorpio we have to look to powerful Pluto, who is right at home in this Sign. Ancient texts wrote of the mighty "hidden" planet that would bring great evolutionary challenges and changes to humankind. Pluto was not "discovered" until 1930. The pace of events began moving into new gear then. The splitting of the atom was a significant Plutonic event, as was the Holocaust. The world was changed forever from the energies unleashed, and humanity is on notice that to evolve to full potential we must learn to use cooperation, not conflict, to solve problems.

The rightful ruler, Pluto, took over Scorpio from Mars, who had been caretaking the Sign until Pluto's advent. Now Pluto's children, Scorpions, have new power and magnetism unavailable for millennia before. This can be seen in the third symbol which Pluto imprinted on the Sign of Scorpio. The most commonly used symbol is the scorpion. This tough little creature, able to withstand searing temperatures and defeat animals many times its size, shows the invincible courage of the Sign. However, the deadly scorpion may sometimes sting for the love of stinging; also depicting the downside of unevolved Scorpio. The second symbol, used throughout time in the more esoteric teachings, is the eagle. Why? Because the eagle is majestic and powerful and able to rise above the dross of the physical world. Now add to these the phoenix, the legendary purple and gold bird which, upon being consumed with fire, will rise from its own ashes. This symbol of immortality and resurrection suits Pluto-governed Scorpio very well, particularly as it integrates the better values of the other two, bringing harmony to the Scorpio nature where before there may have been division.

This fascinating insight into the depths of your little (but powerful!) star should bring helpful enlightenment. The only factor to fear is maltreatment of a Scorpio babe curdling its great love into hate. Needless to say, this is completely out of the question where you and your star child are concerned. Most likely the star spangled fingerprints of great destiny having brought you together as parent and child are quite visible to you. Certainly you are aware of the sacred trust being placed in you as parent to this wondrous little being. You are also finding out what a marvel this child is. The more love, warmth and security you give, the more your mood and needs are intuited, and baby miraculously fits in and flows along with it all, gaining many admirers along the way.

A happy Scorpio babe is a constant source of delight, with a certain twinkle in its little eyes reserved especially for adored and beloved parents. Lovable and friendly, magnetizing much attention its way, your young Scorpio will amaze you with shrewd and surprising reactions to situations and people. As a baby infant Scorpio can be quite content with its own company if secure in your love and knowing you are nearby. As youngsters, swimming and the more inner forms of martial arts such as t'ai chi or aikido, help their natural evolution into the favorable future which awaits them. And throughout, the force of your star child's love for you will be a strength and inspiration. Remember, their love and loyalty once given is an unwavering force. The adult Scorpio will do whatever is necessary to promote parent's welfare. Right down to a quiet word with anyone who's bothering you (you can be sure you'll never see that nuisance again!), to rebuilding the family home and fortunes. (Did we mention the Scorpionic, sometimes miraculous, ability to manifest resources and money?!) With your retirement savings and your adult Scorpio, you won't have to worry about anything!

TO SUMMARIZE: A tiny Scorpio may weigh just a few kilograms, but these little characters have a strength and willpower that belies their small size. Stay firm but kind with them and you will help to turn their considerable powers to constructive use in early life. If they understand they are loved, they will have no problems with confidence.

**MOST IMPORTANT LESSONS:** Compassion and forgiveness.

**SUITABLE VOCATIONS:** Psychiatry, banking and corporate business, healer, detective, military service, artistic catalyst.

### WELL-PARENTED SCORPIONS
Prince Charles * Captain James Cook * The Prophet Mohammed * Joan Sutherland * Jonas Salk * Madame Marie Curie * John Cleese * Whoopi Goldberg * Hillary Rodham Clinton

### NOT SO WELL-PARENTED SCORPIONS
Paul Joseph Goebbels * Senator Joe McCarthy * Dylan Thomas * Marie Antoinette * The Shah of Iran * Pablo Picasso * Emperor Tiberius * Vivien Leigh

# Sagittarius baby

23 November – 22 December

ARCHANGEL: Zadkiel, angel of guidance

BIRTHSTONE: Turquoise

METAL: Tin

COLOR: Royal blue

HERB: Sage

FLOWER: Carnation

TREE: Traditional — Oak

COUNTRIES: Australia, Spain

CITIES: Athens, San Francisco

KNOW THUS FAR FORTH — BY ACCIDENT MOST STRANGE,
BOUNTIFUL FORTUNE. — Shakespeare, *The Tempest*

If your parenting genes are inspired by the notion of an enchanting, active child, one who has providence in large quotas, baby Sagittarius is your match.

This particular Zodiac star is also sometimes known as the "gold card of the Zodiac." Why? Quite simply because of the overwhelming evidence that Sagittarians generally have more of the ability to summon and meet with good luck and fortunate circumstances than the rest of us. (The person who lost their job, and then bought the winning lotto ticket could be a thumbnail sketch of a Sagittarius!) The Sagittarian believes that everyone should have a good life, and their frank, open, yet philosophical approach to life ensures this outcome, in most cases, for them.

Your little Sagittarian star is born under the auspices of generous Jupiter (also known as Zeus, king of the gods in Olympus). This big and bountiful planet has long been associated with luck, good fortune, philosophy and fruitful travel. As the ancients would say, "If Jupiter be in good aspect, success is assured." So, you get the idea. The bottom line of the healthy Sagittarian's attitude to life is optimism and faith, thanks to great Jupiter tending his star children. The majesty and vitality of Jupiter in the night sky attests to this planet's power. Interestingly enough, unlike any of the other planets, Jupiter emits more light and energy than it receives from the Sun. So something is surely going on in this giant planet's relationship with the rest of the universe. And much the same could be said for your tiny star baby.

However, don't make the mistake of thinking, "Great. Choosing infant Sagittarius will change my life, and work like a four leaf clover for me." You know what Shakespeare, the great bard, said, "The best laid plans of mice and men . . . " If the intent is wrong, it will never work. No. You must want baby Sagittarius to love, nurture and enjoy as a delightful and dear little charge from heaven. The more open-hearted you are to your divine star baby, the more you will reap the full glory of baby's inborn potential unfolding.

Bringing this child up is not going to be a waltz through the park, it's going to be more like a sprint around the fairground. But, my word, you are going to have fun and enlightenment in equal doses. Inspiration, exhilaration and lots of laughs. Even when baby is still in the womb, life may take new directions, showing you previously unconsidered dimensions, waking you up to greater things. Walks in the outdoors will also have inspired a great meditative connection between you and baby. The time of delivery will probably be surrounded by amazing and fortuitous synchronicity. When baby Sagittarius is put in your arms not only is parental pride and love instant, but also the feeling of a great friendship between you.

The Sagittarian spirit is an adventuresome one. Your star child needs plenty of room to move but, particularly in the early days, with your ever-watchful eye making sure trouble and danger are kept out of the picture. This star infant knows no fear and would toddle into the lions' den because the big cats looked interesting. (Being Sagittarian, they'd probably toddle out again! But this is not the kind of thing to be left to chance!) An ever-present curiosity keeps your little Sagittarian constantly investigating. Funny, fluffy and brightly colored soft toys, along with ones that squeak and make noises, keep baby Sagittarius merrily amused. As will being outside in the fresh air and being taken on walks with you. When able to walk independently (which these babies tend to achieve quite early — Sagittarians love to head toward new horizons!), a hobby or rocking horse is a great source of enjoyment for them. As is something baby can tow around on a string, like a little trolly or toy on wheels.

Baby Sagittarius usually likes being with other children too. Other kids tend to delight in Sagittarius's company. Your Zodiac star's commanding, cheerful and charismatic qualities become apparent early on. Even adults are affected by baby Sagittarian's special magic. Infant Sagittarians of under two weeks have been known to bring admiring adults to their knees with laughter and awed delight. Jupiter's children have a certain air of sagacity and far-sightedness about them as well, which also tends to strike wonder in others.

This star Sign can be quite "sporty," have a need to expend energy, and a love of wide open spaces. So factor in plenty of outdoor and athletic activity as your Sagittarian grows. Make schooling interesting and pose it as an exciting adventure. Otherwise your Sagittarian will get bored with rote learning, and fidget, as their love of freedom conflicts with being closed in. Don't ever doubt your star child's intelligence. They have that in spades. Teaching which engages your Sagittarian's IQ is the answer.

Sagittarians respect the family principle, but they also like to view their parents as important companions in their wide circle of friends. Even though an adventuresome life may see your Sagittarius offspring be one of the first to leave home, don't doubt that there will be a cameo of you in their hearts. Coming under the auspices of abundant and successful Jupiter means this star Sign can make large amounts of money and achieve a substantial public profile in a variety of ways; sometimes through going into business ventures with parents, but mostly through seizing the gold-plated opportunities life brings them. However, your multi-talented Sagittarian will always share their bounty with beloved parents. Just don't be surprised if they bring all their friends when they come to visit!

TO SUMMARIZE: The Sagittarius trait of loving company shows even when they are babies. They have a fun loving nature and a keen desire for friendship. Make the most of their baby days because this charming, funny, curious little person is likely to be the most independent (and popular!) member of the family, and dislikes being tied down. Their personal charisma will ensure they have a successful life.

**MOST IMPORTANT LESSONS:** Tact and responsibility.

**SUITABLE VOCATIONS:** Travel, law, publishing, explorer, actor or artist, tycoon, minister, politics.

## WELL-PARENTED SAGITTARIANS
Sir Winston Churchill * Tina Turner * Walt Disney * Harpo Marx * William Blake * Jane Fonda * Brad Pitt * Mark Twain * Ludwig van Beethoven

## NOT SO WELL-PARENTED SAGITTARIANS
Nostradamus * Frank Sinatra * Henri de Toulouse-Lautrec * Francisco Franco * Mary, Queen of Scots * Maria Callas * Catherine of Aragon * Nero * Josef Stalin

# Capricorn
## baby

23 December – 20 January

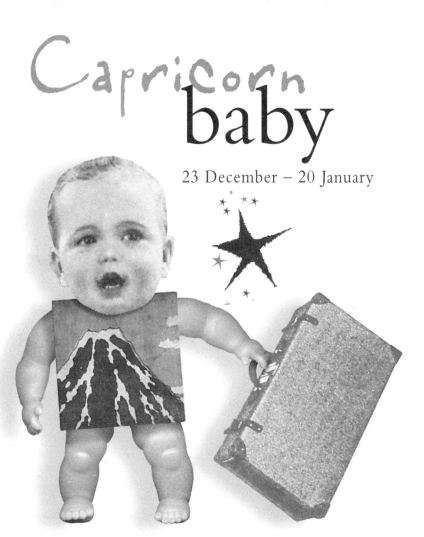

ARCHANGEL: Oriphiel, angel of fundamentals

BIRTHSTONE: Garnet

METAL: Lead

COLOR: Burgundy

HERB: Solomon's seal

FLOWER: Tulip

TREE: Traditional — Pine

COUNTRIES: India, Afghanistan

CITIES: Oxford, Adelaide

BOUND BY MY CHARITY AND MY BLESSED ORDER, I COME TO VISIT THE AFFLICTED SPIRITS ... THAT I MAY MINISTER TO THEM ACCORDINGLY. — Shakespeare, *Measure for Measure*

D oes a complex little bundle of successful but sensitive, independent yet patient, bewitching but sometimes self-doubting character qualities wrapped up in one individual attract your parenting inclinations? Yes? Well baby Capricorn and you will make a great team.

This ambitious, hardworking but charismatic star of the Zodiac has a tender soul. As an infant they need unrestrained amounts of unconditional love and acceptance. Otherwise they will grow up with a crusty exterior in order to prevent others getting near their heartfelt emotions. Because this little Zodiac star departs from heaven bringing much hard-won wisdom with them, and often look older than they are, people mistakenly believe the child is impervious to difficulties and can also handle being downloaded with parental problems. Not so. Little Capricorn only appears that way. And the more baby Capricorn is shunted to one side in order for seemingly more pressing matters to be attended to, the stronger the wall uncomplaining tiny Capricorn erects about them.

This star baby also takes on messages such as being "inferior" and "unlovable" when parenting actions leave a lot to be desired. Patient, responsible little Capricorn simply endures, not wanting to cry and upset parents or the situation any further. Capricorn baby retreats within and, in the worst case scenario, infant Capricorn's health begins to ail. So unfair when, in all likelihood, baby Capricorn tried to cause as little trouble as possible through the pregnancy and delivery process.

You can see how crucial it is to build baby Capricorn's self-esteem and nourish this infant soul's strength through loving and affectionate attention from day one. With this quality of parenting, young Capricorn remains healthy, happy and can grow up to be one of the most successful people on Earth. Establishing loving communication even when baby is still in the womb is a good way to go. Think loving and comforting thoughts to baby during gestation. Speak to your child out loud if that feels right, as baby Capricorn's antennae are always out. Yet another reason to make the pregnancy as happy and stress-free as possible.

The serious side and profound depth to Capricorn has much to do with coming under the governance of solemn and not to be trifled with Saturn. Ancient astrology had great respect, verging on fear, for this planet. The three outer planets were yet to be discovered and Saturn was known as "the ring pass not," All things were circumscribed by and ended in Saturn's orbit. Saturn was also known (and still is) as the "Great Teacher," and the purveyor of strict justice. The karmic balancer. We can also see Saturn as "tough love" par excellence. The kind that will rap the knuckles on the hand reaching, yet again, for the gate which opens onto a busy and dangerous highway. Saturn often saves us from our worst excesses in ways which, at the time, may seem painful. But when we look back we see how much was learned (Great Teacher, remember?), and how fortunate, in the long run, it was that those events occurred. (Saturn can be the master of "blessings in disguise.")

Being the disciplinarian of the Zodiac and teacher of the fundamental laws of life is a highly responsible position. In fact, it is said in older writings that humanity only became able to begin discovery of the transcendental planets in 1781 (Uranus, by William Herschel) thanks to the centuries of schooling (now we were able to progress "beyond the gate") from Saturn. Finally, humankind was out of kindergarten, and able to progress to another grade. And Saturn's load lightened as other planets arrived to assist in the grand plan of humanity's evolution.

Even so, Capricornians, Saturn's children, remain keenly aware of the consequences of wrongdoing. That, ultimately, the piper must be paid. Life is not a free lunch. One must pay one's dues and fulfill obligations. However, the Capricorn star derives great satisfaction from constructively contributing to civilization, and keeping life's books balanced. No shirking duties here. Give your Capricorn a good upbringing and baby will have what it takes to make it into history's pages, for all the right reasons.

It is sometimes said that baby Capricorns look like wise elders, just in miniature form. Certainly when you hold your tiny star for the first time, the wisdom deep in those little eyes will make a significant impact. Baby Capricorn, born with the understanding of arriving into unconditional love, further uplifts the joy experienced. From now it can only get better as you tend to this worthy soul who has chosen you as parent.

In infant days be sure that baby eats well, and gets all the calcium needed to form strong bones and teeth. Make sure to hold and cuddle your little star often, and tell them how much you love them. When well loved and not made to feel insecure, these are very sturdy children. Capricorns have an affinity with crystals. Saturn, their majestic ruler, delights in this form. A crystal here and there in baby's room helps stabilize and calm your star infant's energy, as will happy times in the bath, rusks to chew on when teething and blocks to build with as a toddler.

Do not push your star child to achieve, but do give every support to their success. The Capricorn child suffers if feeling parental expectation is not being lived up to. Never make your child feel inferior. Praise works much better than denigration. Your Capricorn star's superb inborn gifts will then just unfold naturally, unhindered by imposed inhibitions. Musical studies, particularly classical piano, help nourish your developing Capricorn's potential as well.

The adult Capricorn will work hard at success, thanks to the perseverance bestowed by Saturn and, once attained, success will be long-lasting. The "traditionalist" side of Capricorn, also courtesy of Saturn, ensures that parents are looked after lovingly, respectfully and given full honors for their part in Capricorn's prosperity and success. And, no matter what weighty matters may be concerning your progeny or where they may be on the planet, your birthday and all other special dates will be remembered. If you need them, they will be there. Capricornian thrift, or other fortuitous factors, ensures your offspring's bank balance will rise to all occasions too!

**TO SUMMARIZE:** Sometimes little Capricorns look older than they are. But remember, they will retain their good looks throughout their life. These babies also have a wisdom beyond their years, often to the surprise of their parents. Their great capacity for organization enables them to surmount all obstacles and achieve their goals in life. The love given to them in their infant years provides the confidence to do so.

**MOST IMPORTANT LESSONS:** Humour and self-value.

**SUITABLE VOCATIONS:** Politician, architect, CEO of large company, movie producer or star, scientist, musician, police officer, dentist.

## WELL-PARENTED CAPRICORNS

Sir Isaac Newton * Elvis Presley * Maggie Smith * Muhammad Ali * Humphrey Bogart * Dr. Albert Schweitzer * Princess Michael of Kent * Cary Grant * Joan of Arc * Martin Luther King * Rowan Atkinson

## NOT SO WELL-PARENTED CAPRICORNS

Richard Nixon * Edgar Allan Poe * Federico Fellini * Benedict Arnold * Conrad Hilton * Mao Zedong * Marlene Dietrich * Al Capone * Aristotle Onassis

# Aquarius baby

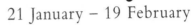

21 January – 19 February

ARCHANGEL: Ariel, angel of air

BIRTHSTONE: Amethyst

METAL: Uranium

COLOR: Purple

HERB: Elderberry

FLOWER: Orchid

TREE: Traditional — Elm

COUNTRIES: Sweden, Canada

CITIES: Sydney, Moscow

I THINK THE KING IS BUT A MAN, AS I AM; THE VIOLET SMELLS TO HIM AS IT DOTH TO ME. — Shakespeare, *Henry V*

I f you're considering parenting a friendly, determined, intellectual and unique cherub, then baby Aquarius is most definitely your babe.

But you must be open-minded and forward-thinking to successfully parent this particular star of the Zodiac. Aquarius is renowned for producing the great inventors and innovators of our time. Revolutionary thinkers, scientific geniuses and inspiring humanitarians flourish in the Sign of Aquarius. Computers and technology owe their birth to this Sign. Democracy also owes its origins to Aquarius.

Aquarius has always been the Sign of ideas and higher aspirations, as well as the progress and evolution of humanity as a whole. However, with the arrival of mighty Uranus in 1781 (confirmed "discovered" by William Herschel on the night of 13 March), the true ruler of Aquarius (its advent having been written of in ancient texts), all of the above really began to kick off. (Serious Saturn had been caretaking Aquarius up until this time and, although glad to relinquish this task and attend solely to Capricorn, still retains an affinity with this Sign. Without the disciplined application Saturn provides, how many ideas, scientific or otherwise, would have made it into three dimensional form?!) The French Revolution, founding the modern democratic process, and the Industrial Revolution launching technology, quickly followed. Cosmic Uranus was here and happening, taking humanity into the coming Age of Aquarius. The unabated advance of technology has transformed the world we humans know. It is a new era. The Age of Aquarius has dawned. Cyberspace is a rudimentary symbol of this. Electric consciousness encircles the globe, connecting the human family as never before.

But back to your family specifically. By now it has probably become obvious that the Aquarian star child is one who needs the freedom that comes from not being stereotyped or boxed in by others' expectations. The more the Aquarius star is able to march to the beat of its own drum, the more the inborn missions within are able to develop and play out. The rebellion factor is also considerably negated because there are no false structures to bust out of. Being able to accept the uniqueness of your Aquarian babe with loving delight ensures their trajectory into the stratosphere of where your star child is going to make a difference. One that will benefit all.

Consciousness is the name of the game wherever Aquarius is concerned. Along with this comes certain levels of intuition and telepathy. This can result in feeling there is much communication between you during pregnancy. (In fact, if there is any problem during gestation, you can ask for baby's help in sorting it out!) And after birth, your Aquarian angel and you feel blissfully united as you rest together. You know you share a special destiny.

Sometimes the Aquarian star baby does not take to conventional infant fare. It may be that your child prefers soy milk to dairy milk, for example. So don't be afraid to experiment in finding what nutrition serves baby best. Another factor important to your star baby's development is truth. Aquarians know when they are being fed lies, and it twists them up. Aquarians detect falsehood instantly and, because they *know* truth is the basis for a united humanity, tend to feel more and more isolated the longer this state of affairs continues.

But your little one will never have to put up with patronizing platitudes or any other glib attempts to coerce them to accept what is fundamentally untrue. Instead, your Aquarian star will have all questions answered with appropriate truths, and be surrounded by genuine love as an infant. A planetary mobile above the crib, or one of spaceships, can keep your baby amused. This babe tends to take to crazy looking soft toys too, and a space-age rattle or similar will suit your star child down to the ground. Don't worry if your little star doesn't conform to usual baby routines. Together you'll work out a rhythm of feeding, sleeping and playing. (A well-ventilated nursery makes your Aquarian star feel more at home too.) Aquarians are different, and forcing the "square peg into a round hole" syndrome on them is destructive indeed. They do hear the reverberations of a different drum, and you have to allow that.

This doesn't mean that your Aquarian star child should be allowed to run riot. Not at all. Wise parental guidance, with the best interests of the child at heart, is what is required. But if your Aquarius asks to learn tap dancing when it's ballet for everyone else, or play basketball instead of cricket, then you should permit it. Remember, what may seem little idiosyncrasies are often the seeds of great genius where Aquarians are concerned. This is an intelligent Sign. (Although often they draw understanding directly from the cosmic mind, and can have little patience with regimented learning. The Steiner Schools' philosophy is one that has the required latitude to nurture the Aquarian intellect.) Aquarius is also a determined Sign (goals, even long-term ones, are pursued with great tenacity). Loving acceptance pushes confusion out of the picture, allowing your Aquarian to forge on with natural development of their unique abilities. Talking things out and over with your young Aquarian is the sure-fire way to resolve any differences of opinion that may arise.

As babies, Aquarians are usually confidently charming at family get-togethers or celebrations, even if strangers are present. With that inborn sense of the brother and sisterhood of humanity, your electric little star is friendly and willing to give anyone a chance. Sociable and amicable, little Aquarius is usually quite a hit. Baby's attractive little face, with fantastic, far-seeing eyes engages the attention of others, and your baby's command of the moment will thrill everyone. Family history and legend will be made as, somehow, the presence of baby Aquarius adds immensely to the event. It could be something like the cranky old relative who, when brushed by tiny Aquarius's big all-loving and all-knowing aura, changes forever for the better. (Possibly leaving a large legacy for little Aquarius too!) Or a tense situation may be quelled by toddler Aquarius tottering into the potential arena, surveying all, then saying, "Better now?" The list could go on. Your Aquarian child is phenomenal in bringing just what the moment needs. These cosmic sprites are surrounded by many angels.

The Aquarian understanding that, fundamentally, all humans are linked in one big kinship of family translates in personal domestic life as the desire to do the right thing by parents, along with a deep-seated love. You have been through much together and your adult Aquarian appreciates this. There's a dedication to your well-being and happiness. Your Aquarian scion's ingenious and inventive nature can solve any parental problems, and bring you great satisfaction through meeting with unusual success. But then you knew your Aquarian star was destined for this anyway.

TO SUMMARIZE: Every parent believes their child to be in some way unique. In the case of Aquarius babies, they are 100 percent correct! Each free-spirited Aquarian is one of a kind, so don't expect them to conform, just enjoy observing their development. Popular and confident, but detached, they will stride toward an original and exciting future.

MOST IMPORTANT LESSONS: Diplomacy and discrimination.

**SUITABLE VOCATIONS:** Rocket science, humanitarian activities, airline industry, alternative medicine, international affairs, reporter, inventor, any field on the cutting edge of humanity's advance.

## WELL-PARENTED AQUARIANS

Abraham Lincoln ✳ Charles Darwin ✳ Anna Pavlova ✳ Banjo Paterson ✳ Charles Dickens ✳ Oprah Winfrey ✳ Galileo Galilei ✳ Lord Byron ✳ Nicolaus Copernicus ✳ Clark Gable ✳ Jane Seymour

## NOT SO WELL-PARENTED AQUARIANS

James Dean ✳ Benny Hill ✳ Tallulah Bankhead ✳ W. Somerset Maugham ✳ Havelock Ellis ✳ Bertolt Brecht ✳ Virginia Woolf ✳ James Joyce ✳ Jackson Pollock ✳ Wolfgang Amadeus Mozart ✳ Nell Gwynne

# Pisces baby

20 February – 20 March

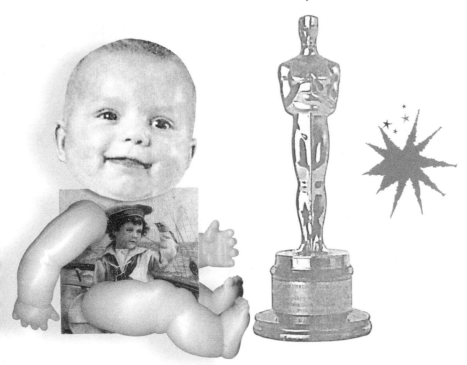

ARCHANGEL: Metatron, angel of illumination

BIRTHSTONE: Moonstone

METAL: Platinum

COLOR: Lilac

HERB: Bilberry

FLOWER: Waterlily

TREE: Traditional — Birch

COUNTRIES: Portugal, Tibet

CITIES: Alexandria, Auckland

THOU WAST, THAT DID PRESERVE ME! THOU DIDST SMILE, INFUSED WITH A FORTITUDE FROM HEAVEN. — Shakespeare, *The Tempest*

If a congenial, adaptable and versatile child, one also supplied with ample allotments of fascinating magnetism and artistry, pushes your parenting genes, then baby Pisces is undoubtedly your wish fulfilled.

However, there is a certain fragility to the Piscean star which you have to address with loving attention from day one. (Some say this comes from being the last Sign on the Zodiac wheel and therefore being that much closer to heaven in general. The theory is that all the preceding Signs have been traversed, great lessons distilled from each, giving vast depth and dimension to the Piscean soul. Some even say this is the Sign that is the step-off point to permanent sainthood!) A good analogy here is the horticultural scientific investigation into the effect of music on rose-growing. One group of rose bushes had nothing but heavy metal music played continuously, the other nothing but classical harmonies. The first group not only grew miserably and deformed, but quite a few plants died. Whereas all members of the second group flourished, and put forth beautiful blooms. That, dear prospective parent, quite graphically describes the effect the vibrations of this physical realm can have on the sensitive soul of the Piscean star. Now that you are very clearly aware of this situation you are ready to take on the divine mission that having a Piscean babe entails, and will *always* ensure nothing but love, assurance and affirmation reign around your little angel.

Your little minnow Piscean's descent into the sea of life comes from great trust in you, beloved parent. They have launched out of heaven and into your domain, because it has been shown that you have the caliber that will keep the deep soul of your Piscean babe not only intact, but also nurtured. Not tattered, damaged or twisted, as could so easily happen to this precious jewel visiting planet Earth in order to make it a better place. Quite possibly magic, miracles and, perhaps, some testing occurred around the conception and gestation period. But the "magic" and "miracles" are what should prevail, especially if you employ meditation and positive affirmations during this time. In fact, use of these practices will see you and your blessed angel experience a divine and loving birth, beautifully uniting you forever.

The sometimes "otherworldly" qualities and mesmerizing fascination baby Pisces impresses all with (without even trying! — this is just the way they are) has much to do with mysterious and mystical Neptune, who watches over his Piscean children from on high. Jovial Jupiter took care of the Piscean star tribe until Neptune's (the second transcendental planet to arrive, and the prophesied ruler of Pisces) "discovery" in 1846. Although now free to devote more attention to his Sagittarius children, Jupiter still retains strong affinity with Pisces. Luck and mirth are what he lends to this Sign. Neptune brought a new dimension to Pisces, as well as new principles for humankind to begin working and evolving with. The rise of psychology, photography, film, pharmaceuticals and spiritualism are just some of the events Neptune launched into the human sphere. Unified compassion was also catalyzed by Neptune, resulting in the final abolition of the slave trade.

The rapid rise of "spiritualism" in the latter part of the nineteenth century, although primitive, did allow people to experiment with their relationship to the divine, without restrictions of dogma and rigid beliefs. And this brings us to the essence of the principle which Neptune symbolizes — that of divine love, the ceaseless force that is in continual creation of the universe and which, in turn, unites us with the ever-expanding universe. For those with a little knowledge of the chakras, Neptune is known as Kether, the crown chakra blossoming at the top of the head.

All the above quite definitely spells out the profound vulnerability, but also the invincible strength, your Piscean babe is born with. The compassionate heart, the deeply sensitive soul thrust onto this harsh Earth plane can be needlessly wounded and even scarred for life by ugly and negative vibrations being the norm of daily existence. What a terrible tragedy and waste. A little being incarnate to bring love, ending up crippled by the very forces it came to help elevate. It must also be said here that a damaged Piscean can exact highly clever and painful revenges.

Now that you are clearly in the know, dear parent, your star child will grow and develop, free of any kind of trauma, into a fine and wonderful human being who has considerable greatness to offer our planet and civilization. You're already highly aware that baby Pisces must not be subject to bad or discordant energy. If you feel your little star is uncomfortable with someone, it doesn't matter who it is, do not force your baby to stay in that person's arms in a misguided effort to get baby used to it. Do not prop your sweet little infant in front of the television. They may only be a few weeks old, but the images, noise, chaos and mayhem wreak havoc on the tiny Piscean system. Instead, make sure baby's room is bright and fresh, with interesting pastel motifs and is well-aired. A little aquarium in your star baby's line of vision will be very soothing too. As will lovely ambient music (Pachelbel's *Canon* combined with ocean surf must have been composed with baby Pisces in mind!), plus lullabies and warm cuddles from you. Fairy tales and stories from King Arthur's time will also wonderfully nourish your star child's powerful and creative imagination. And that is the heart of the matter — to plant nothing but good, wholesome and loving seeds while your Piscean child is young. You don't have to worry about "toughening them up," because the invincible strength in their souls evolves alongside the development of their destined potential.

The Piscean child is alive to the arts. So painting, music, and enjoyment of the grandeur of sky and sea nurture their spirit. Just always be there for your Pisces star; be their rock and your child will grow into a remarkable individual. One who will also deeply revere and love treasured parents. Your adult Pisces, whether tycoon or sailor, will always find the time and wherewithal to lovingly see to your needs.

**TO SUMMARIZE:** Piscean babies seem to have come from some mythical place, with their dreamy eyes and magical aura. It is true, they are sensitive souls, but good parenting and loving helps them deal most successfully with the world, as well as retain their very special qualities. Their vivid imaginations and graceful personalities inspire others.

**MOST IMPORTANT LESSONS:** Concentration and artistic expression.

**SUITABLE VOCATIONS:** Film, dance, fashion design, seer, beauty and modelling industries, strategist, psychologist, marine biologist, navy.

## WELL-PARENTED PISCEANS

Frederick Chopin * Prince Edward * Elizabeth Taylor * Albert Einstein * George Harrison * Kiri Te Kanawa * Rudolf Nureyev * Michelangelo * Mikhail Gorbachev

## NOT SO WELL-PARENTED PISCEANS

Jack Kerouac ✳ Laurence Durrell ✳ Jean Harlow ✳ Vaslav Nijinsky ✳ V. A. Molotov ✳ Gloria Vanderbilt ✳ Peter Fonda ✳ L. Ron Hubbard ✳ Zeppo Marx

# Star parents

Ancient Rome had an annual feast called

PARENTALIA to commemorate ancestors and

venerate parents. Good parents deserve such

respect today.

# Parentus
## Aries

21 March – 20 April

ONE ATTRACTS MORE BEES WITH HONEY THAN VINEGAR. — Ancient
Egyptian proverb

A s an instant, have to have it NOW! person it could be thought that parenthood, with all its accompanying dues, would not be your cup of tea. But surprise, surprise! Ariens are up there with the best of star parents.

Being the brave, courageous Sign that you are, once you have decided you wish to have a child, nothing will daunt you from achieving this end. Whatever steps are necessary will be taken, and you'll prepare your body for baby's conception and arrival, as well as a nursery!

However, you must be highly aware that your newborn, especially in infancy, will place some restraint on your mobility and freedom of action. It will have to be "baby first," not "me first." Otherwise you could become cranky and impatient as you shuffle through a couple of sleepless nights. But putting your legendary energy and enthusiasm into raising your tiny star will bring untold joy as each unique milestone is reached (first grin, tooth, step and so on), and you valuably participate in your child's character and personality development. You and your special little angel will embark on a wonderful adventure together.

Aries parents are a child's delight in the way that they can quickly pack up for an impromptu holiday or sports event. Also in the way that they are perfectly happy to include their little one in everything. See that person rockclimbing with a baby on board in a backpack? That's an Aries parent. That jogger in the park pushing an infant stroller is another Aries parent. The one in the group singing around the campfire holding a baby is definitely another. But don't think these Zodiac parents take careless risks. Not a bit of it. Baby's safety and well-being will have been thought out to the last detail by their mentally alert parent, and we can be sure baby will be having a wonderful time.

Nothing is too much trouble for the Aries parent where their progeny's schooling, sports activities or future is concerned. Your team is playing far afield next Saturday? No problem. Your Aries parent will get you there with time to spare, and you'll have had a rousing good time on the way. You'll leap out of the (probably 4WD) family vehicle feeling enthused, motivated and ready to go!

Aries parents are absolutely marvellous motivators. Their boundless energy infuses megawatts of achieving power into their offspring as well. However, there is a fine line between firing up ambition and frying confidence. Therefore, the Aries parent must remain sensitive to the impact their mode of encouragement is having on the child. "You can do much better than that" works completely differently if forcefully spoken rather than shouted, and followed up with constructive advice, as well as praise.

The Aries parent usually has a great sense of fun, as well as being athletic and sporty. The vocation of being a parent is taken seriously, but they are not above joining in games or initiating spontaneous exciting events. The quest to provide only the best for their child usually begins from day one. The little newborn feels warm and safe in the ardent love their parent welcomes them with. What a wonderful start! However, to keep this splendid state of affairs on a continual and ascending track, the Aries parent must remember to be wary of imposing their own desires and ambitions onto their precious charge. Listening closely to gauge where your child is really at is always a good idea. This will save many tears and unnecessary misunderstandings, as well as ensure your parent–child relationship only gets better and better.

PROGENY'S ADDENDUM: Being the child of an Aries can bring great advantages. This star progenitor is not only capable of fierce commitment to parenthood, but also tends to remain quintessentially young at heart. A grand combination which brings both security (you know that not only are you well provided for, but your Aries parent will also brave burning fires to rescue you) and delicious merriment when that impish child kicks in (remember the Christmas you had to wrestle your presents from said parent, and poor Aunt Sally's new scarf was found on the cat?!). Home was always an exciting place when your Aries parent was around. The zip and crackle of their monumental energy lit up life for everyone — even your friends, as your generous-hearted progenitor always made sure to include them in the fun whenever possible.

The famed and potent Aries charisma (songs are still sung about Arian King of Scotland, Robert Bruce, almost seven hundred years since — and some people even believe he plans to return!) also blesses you. Through pure force of personality, this star parent can wheedle you the last seat on the roller coaster or place in your course of choice at university. And the ardent and vital nature of your Aries star parent has inspired you to be the best you can; even now, the love and admiration you have for your parent continues to expand. As an adult, you still thoroughly enjoy time spent with your vibrant parent — although you do sometimes testily question why legions of others seem to spring to attention on sighting your star parent and demand to join in on the action. You should just accept that commanding Mars always ensures this reaction to Aries, as well as providing bags of initiative to keep your star parent's popularity fires burning. As you've experienced, many great opportunities can come to light for you because of this, so don't try to fence your Aries star parent in.

## POSITIVE ARIEN KEYWORDS
Inspirational * Talented * Admirable

## NOT SO POSITIVE ARIAN KEYWORDS
Impatient * Impetuous * Selfish

## GOOD ARIES PARENT EXAMPLE

Ceres, who searched for, found and rescued her daughter, Proserpine, from the realm of Hades.

## POOR ARIES PARENT EXAMPLE

Hera, who threw her newborn son Hephaestus from Mount Olympus.

# Parentus
## Taurus

21 April – 20 May

IF YOU KNOW THE GREAT AND PRECIOUS, WHERE CAN YOU GO AND NOT SUCCEED? — Lao-tsu

This most worthy Sign of the Zodiac has all the qualities required for successful parenting, in abundance. In fact, "abundance" is one of the keywords associated with Taurus. If you have ever had the good fortune to be invited to dine at a Taurean's table, you'll know exactly what I mean. This star is a firm believer in "too much is better than not enough," and errs (if that's the correct term!) on the side of plentitude. Great food and fine wines, as well as most amiable and agreeable company, are what you are blessed with upon receipt of a Taurean invitation.

This slight digression may be forgiven as filling in a little more of the warm, giving nature of the Taurus star when it comes to nurturing (also known as the "green thumb" Sign of the Zodiac; indoor plants to plantations thrive under a dedicated Taurean's ministrations). "Ample" is a word Taureans resonate with. To this Zodiac tribe it means that there is plenty to go round, and no one is left out. And this is critically important to the Taurean star. Why? Because when their word is given on any matter, the follow through is 100 percent. "Commitment" is another strong word for Taureans. Which is why a Taurean may ruminate for some time before deciding to become a parent. There is a strong need to be absolutely sure there will be the emotional and material resources needed for quality parenting. This should be respected. Let your Taurean take all the time required to come to a comfortable decision. Besides, because this star makes a natural parent, their pull will be toward wanting a child, and because this is a "fertile" Sign, conception should be relatively problem-free.

It is highly important not to push your Taurean for answers. Not only will this hamper the decision process, but could also backfire in one of the famous bull rages. The normally placid Taurean can only be pushed so far and, when that line is crossed, watch out for getting the fright of your life — especially when something as deep and sensitive as becoming a parent is being considered by this deep and sensitive Sign.

However, once decided upon parenthood, it will be all systems go. Concerted effort will be put into achieving the desired aim of a child, plus a stable world to support the tiny new human being. And what a fortunate babe to be put into the arms of a Taurean star parent! Warm, solid love surrounds the infant, who senses immediately the security it has been born into, and relaxes into beaming love back. The wonderful sense of being right at home is made even more so by the sound of the dulcet Taurean tones warming the little one's ear.

Because of turning everything over during the process of decision-making, the Taurean is ready for the demands and changes parenthood brings. Even if the Taurus star enters parenthood by "accident" (although it's said, particularly in this instance, there is no such thing — simply destiny seizing its chance) as it were, they will still be prepared to parent. After all, this Sign has a strong bond with Mother Earth, and knows the endurance, fortitude and love needed to foster life. The Taurean star also instinctively knows the great and priceless joys that will accompany such level of care.

From the beginning, the little newborn knows they've got it made as their Taurean parent cares for them with tender patience, accompanied by the ability to stick to a reliable routine. No feeding times forgotten here by the parent having been distracted by seemingly more important or exciting events. Enchanting lullabies, enthralling tales and yummy sustenance are other areas where the Taurean parent excels. But don't think this star parent is a pushover. Not a bit of it! They know when and where to put their foot down.

**PROGENY'S ADDENDUM:** A Taurus parent is a child's rock. Throughout all life's turbulent events and turning points, right into adulthood, the Taurean's scion can rely on the love, common sense, strength and reliability of their parent. You may have grown up in a slightly ramshackle house, with pets and stray people dotted here and there. The garden may have resembled a small jungle, but gee — it was fun to play in. And friends were always welcome under the family roof and at the dinner table. You wouldn't swap your Taurean parent for the whole world!

However, you do often wonder why it is that others instantly listen up and gaze, charmed and mesmerized, at your star progenitor on first meeting and thereafter. This is because of the honey tones with which harmonious and gracious Venus imbues the Taurean voice and aura. Your star parent has wrought many miracles for you through the spoken magic of their words, so thank them for it.

## POSITIVE TAUREAN KEYWORDS
Trustworthy * Compassionate * Foresighted

## NOT SO POSITIVE TAUREAN KEYWORDS
Stubborn * Complacent * Jealous

## GOOD TAURUS PARENT EXAMPLE
Inachus, whose love for his daughter, Io, resulted in the reversing of a spell which had turned her into a heifer.

## POOR TAURUS PARENT EXAMPLE
Venus, who instructed her son, Cupid, to shoot his love arrow where it would cause most mischief.

# Parentus
## Geminus

21 May – 21 June

THINK AS THOUGH YOUR THOUGHTS WERE WRITTEN ON THE SKY
IN FIRE. FOR IN TRUTH THEY ARE. — Zoroaster

In terms of motherhood or fatherhood, it may come as a surprise to some that Geminians can perform extremely well. "But . . . (*splutter, splutter*). . . " I can hear the more flabbergasted among you begin, "what about their love of freedom, loathing of being pinned down, and extremely active social life?! Would they give all that away?" The short answer is yes, and no.

As that reply in itself is not very helpful, further elaboration on the subject is obviously required. First, remember this star of the Zodiac is as multi-faceted as a prism; and second, as multi-skilled as a potato peeling egg-boiler. Geminis can face anything and deal with anything, except boredom. If the Gemini star makes a conscious decision to have a child (remember, this is one highly intelligent Sign), you can be sure the whole matter has been profoundly deliberated upon, even if at lightning speed. Therefore, they know what's entailed and consider themselves up to it.

Making a great parent is one of their facets, and rearing children well is just another expression of their talented nature. The Gemini star would not undertake parenthood lightly either. After making that decision, or if discovering a child was due, Gemini will almost instantly begin reading and researching the whys and wherefores of the little miracle developing in the womb, as well as the art of parenting. Prenatal classes will be attended, seen as a valuable arc on the learning curve, and the best baby gear and nursery paraphernalia carefully thought out.

It should be mentioned, however, that in general Geminians do better with a good stretch of being footloose and fancy-free behind them before tackling the parental role. Without having had the chance to explore the world around them (much in the way a butterfly does — no ties — simply dancing through the blue sky and being made welcome by all the wonderful flowers the joyful lepidopteron decides to visit), the Gemini star can feel somewhat caged, mournfully wondering what has been missed out on. But, having been able to stretch their wings enables the Gemini to weave a great sunny overview into their parenting mode. They have connected to the bigger picture and have the vision to guide their own child in finding the right place within it.

But, paradoxically, some Geminis become parents early on. Often in their teens. What happens in these cases is that child and parent grow together. The young Gemini parent will work hard at doing all the right things (and they will succeed — Gemini is a very competent Sign), then when child becomes fledgling adult launched into the world, the (usually under 40 years) parent launches into an exciting life of their own. (Part of this new life comes from other interests this ingenious star parent has pursued alongside parenting.) Needless to say, both parent and child are also great friends, moreover a friendship which ripens further as the years go by.

Don't forget that members of the Gemini Zodiac star tribe are equipped with a finely tuned and highly active central nervous system. The bottom line for all those synaptic gaps firing productively and neurons humming helpfully is sleep. Lots of it. Eight hours a night is best. This can be somewhat of a conundrum for the Gemini star, who finds everything so interesting that bed can be the last thing that beckons. However, when preparing for birth, then parenting, restful slumber is a must. Time for rests should be factored into the day during the gestation process, and catnaps are the order in early parenting, especially when there are nights of broken sleep. Then this magical and resourceful star's radiance will not dim, but continue to light up everyone's world.

PROGENY'S ADDENDUM: As the offspring of a Gemini you will have a childhood rich in tales, along with many memorable events. It may not have been a completely conventional upbringing, but hey — being taken off to the coast of Amalfi when you're two isn't really so bad! And how you loved those stories! If there were no books on hand, or all the fairy tales and Brothers Grimm stories had been read aloud with your parent's unique style of narration, then you'd be treated to a thrilling tale created in the moment by your Gemini parent. They talked with you from the beginning too, and it wasn't long before you were talking back! Great conversations which brought much discovery were common. Your Gemini parent instilled a love of culture in you, without even really trying. The atmosphere you were brought up in did that.

Schooling was another major focus in your house — along with many lighthearted moments too! In fact, you may have been enrolled in pre-school, even high school, before you were born! Help with homework, extra tuition and encouragement were always forthcoming from your Gemini star parent. You know you owe much of your success to them, and love them dearly, but when will people realize this star person is your parent not your sibling?! (Sorry — this is the sign of youth, after all.)

## POSITIVE GEMINI KEYWORDS
Friendly * Perceptive * Versatile

## NOT SO POSITIVE GEMINI KEYWORDS
Critical * Irritable * Restless

## GOOD GEMINI PARENT EXAMPLE
Aeacus, whose faith and intelligence restored his kingdom, enabling Telamon, his son, to throw open the gates and say, "Father, approach and behold things surpassing even your hopes."

## POOR GEMINI PARENT EXAMPLE

Morgana Le Fay, whose clever poisoning of her son Mordred's attitude toward King Arthur made him the fatal instrument in the fall of Camelot.

# Parentus
## Cancerius

22 June – 23 July

Cancerians are the natural-born parents of the Zodiac. When children themselves, the Cancer star was very likely to be the one who brought home all the strays or orphaned wild life to be tended to. They probably had lots of fun playing "house," making mud pies and telling others how things were to be done as well. An eye would have been kept on friends' well-being so that, if things were not as they should be, nurturing Cancer would have stepped in to save the day, and rouse said friend or friends to constructive action. Little Cancer was, in all likelihood, totally devoted to his or her parents — and probably still is! It's clear to see that the basic Cancerian nature is one with all the optimum qualities for great parenting and carrying on family tradition.

However, with emotions as deep as the oceans, and responsive to the mysterious magnetism of the Moon, the Cancer star needs rock-solid security, both material and love-wise, for truly successful parenting. Otherwise problems can become magnified out of proportion or the Cancerian becomes prey to strange fancies that turn calm seas into disturbing raging torrents. None of this is good for parent or child. Which is why things should be talked over thoroughly with your Cancerian before taking the parental plunge. This can be a little more difficult than it sounds. Why? Because the Cancerian star is drawn to mothering or fathering, and is usually highly fertile, thus they can fall into parenting quickly, and early on. Often there is simply no time for the rational element to operate. However, it should be said that, even in these cases, the Cancerian parent will manage, somehow or other, despite depth-charged emotions, to do their best by the child. The Cancer star's urge to parent is primal.

There is no doubt that Cancerians make the best of parents, but with dependable security they make a much better job of it. Without the worry of finding finances for the next water bill, for example, this star Sign is able to express the fundamental, wholesome Cancerian loving and nurturing nature within which children thrive. But when fearful insecurity clouds the picture, great love can become smother love, and the Cancer star becomes somewhat crabby and snappy. Also, a mothering Cancer's usually abundant flow of breast milk can dry up, depriving both she and infant of essential loving contact. Having painted the worst case scenario for our potential Cancerian parents here, whether Mother or Father, the circumstances that could blight their otherwise peerless parenting skills will never have the opportunity to arise. The Cancerian's partner now knows the utmost importance of emotional and physical surety within which to cradle this star's superb parenting power, even if the Cancerian does not.

These stars of the Zodiac usually have somewhat, even if intermittent, spookily psychic proclivities which tell them quite profoundly what is right and what is wrong. So your Cancer parent probably deep down knows exactly the conditions necessary for flourishing child rearing — it's just hard to say so when the desire for a little babe to hold and love is so strong.

And the tiny new infant delivered to a stable and happy Cancerian is a blessed babe indeed. During the gestation period child-to-be and parent are probably sounding each other out. The famous Cancerian psychic (they "feel things" — another good reason for ensuring wholesome and happy vibes surround your Cancerian) faculties tend to come to the fore when life shaping events like pregnancy are in the air or happening. When the newborn is in their Cancer parent's arms, it will be as though they have known each other forever.

As alluded to before, there's something archetypal about Cancerians and parenting. Whether Mother or Father, they instinctively know what to do. The baby's needs are anticipated, nothing is too much trouble, and the little one is reared in a sea of love, care and calm. (About the only word of caution to the Cancerian parent here is not to be so intensely focused on the child that all others, including the partner, become blocked out.)

PROGENY'S ADDENDUM: As an infant, you will have quickly discovered your star parent's talents when it comes to food and home-making. The house didn't only look good, it was also highly comfortable and functional; the sofa was almost as comfy as the parental bosom you rested your little head on! There was no lack of cuddles when you were growing up; if upset you headed straight for the safe arms of your Cancerian parent. Wonderful aromas drifted from the well-equipped kitchen or barbecue as your star parent cooked up a storm. Amazing discussions were had around the dinner table, and great fun on family excursions. Sometimes you weren't sure what your Cancer star parent was going to do next, as they tended to go a bit loopy around full Moon time. But the surprises always ended up bringing great cheer to you and the household. Secretly you felt a little superior to and sorry for those without a Cancer parent — and still do!

## POSITIVE CANCER KEYWORDS
Sympathetic * Industrious * Protective

## NOT SO POSITIVE CANCER KEYWORDS
Moody * Bossy * Possessive

## GOOD CANCER PARENT EXAMPLE
Ulysses, who feigned madness to avoid the Trojan War by ploughing salt into the earth, but turned the plough aside when his infant son, Telemachus, was placed in front of it.

## POOR CANCER PARENT EXAMPLE
Henry VIII, who cast aside his daughter, Elizabeth, after executing her mother, Anne Boleyn.

# Parentus

## LeonuS

24 July – 23 August

LIVE YOUR BELIEFS AND YOU CAN TURN THE WORLD AROUND.
— Henry David Thoreau

Can the Leonine star make a good parent? The short answer is — you bet! Observe the constancy of the Sun rising and setting every day, casting beams of life-giving light onto planet Earth, and there's your model of the Leo parent. Like their celestial ruling body, the Leonine stamina and commitment to life-promoting projects, such as the arts, chefing and family lineage, is legendary. From modern day royals to the ancient Egyptians, and before, Leos feature as patriarchs and matriarchs. The Leo star has an inbuilt urge to propagate their royal genes.

However, this urge can be masked by an urge to propagate themselves! Why? Complete involvement in an artistic career, where they are the "star," or an out of order ego that cannot see beyond its own glory, can abrogate this parental star's fire. Most Leos are more balanced than this, and do desire a chubby cub or two to lead through life's jungle onto the savannahs of success. And even those Leos of the aforementioned ilk tend to wake up after or around forty and pursue having a child of their own with unmitigated zeal.

All the above having been spelled out, it should also be made very clear that this Sun-governed Sign should not be pushed into parenting via such pressures as being labelled "selfish," or being told "you owe it to the family" and so on. No, this basically sunny-natured individual must make the decision unbadgered by unnecessary flak. Such needling and pushing could arouse great obstinacy and completely defeat the purpose. Plus, more than a few Leos need a stretch of shining solo in the Sun before wanting their progeny beside them. But reaching that point is almost a certainty, hence it is "unnecessary" to heckle a lion about child rearing, and it does more damage than good.

So respect your Leo and allow them to come around to parenting in their own good time. Mind you, calendars featuring prides of lions or fetching cherubs will work subliminally on your Leo star's innate desire to propagate and parent. On the other hand, many Leos view parenthood as a vocation and willingly take on that commitment quite early in life. But in each and every case, big-hearted Leo will love their offspring ferociously, and everything necessary for the child's well-being will be done.

During the gestation process, whether the Leo is potential Mater or Pater, a daily walk around the block will keep that heart healthily pumping, as well as work out the spine and skeletal structure. Being a lazy lion and gorging on rich foods can strain the heart and load stress on the back during this time. As this star Sign's natural state is one of buoyant good health, it seems a little silly to damage its optimum state through lack of very simple effort, especially when birthing and the night shifts are coming up.

The Leonine star tribe has a penchant for nothing but the very best. Well, lucky partner, you know! After all, they chose you.

However, that means it is highly unlikely that the Leo star parent will settle for anything second-hand or hand-me-down for their beloved babe. Instead, expect designer christening gowns, along with the premier delivery suite and a deluxe nursery. This is not for show, well, mostly not — the Leo star genuinely believes (and probably rightly so) that they are worthy only of what comes from the top shelf, a belief which extends to cherished children as well. A healthy bank balance certainly smoothes the way for uncomplicated Leo parenting. However, it should be said, that in those cases where the bottom line is not so robust, as long as the love is rich and deep, the Leo star can excel under a trimmed budget. As gold is the metal of these star people, Leos usually manage to attract the necessary funds at the necessary times.

PROGENY'S ADDENDUM: Your Leo parent fought tooth and nail to ensure you had a happy and fruitful childhood. As a newborn babe you sensed the strength of the heartfelt love emanating from your Leo parent, and felt at home immediately. You enjoyed the troops of visitors coming to pay court, and basked in your star parent's evident pride. Home may not have been a castle but, to the child of a Leo parent, many times it felt like one. Then there was the rough and tumble — just as families of lions gambol around and play, so did yours. And just as the lion is there for its cub, and woe betide any creature approaching with harm in mind, so your Leo parent was there for you. Their enthusiasm and belief in you has helped make you the successful adult you are today, and even now your treasured Leo parent is there in a bound, should you call on them. Yes, the limelight always finds said parent, but haven't they always shared it with you from day one?!

## POSITIVE LEO KEYWORDS
Noble * Generous * Protective

## NOT SO POSITIVE LEO KEYWORDS
Domineering * Self-centered * Intolerant

## GOOD LEO PARENT EXAMPLE
Zeus, who granted Pollux's wish to share his immortality with Castor, thus saving his brother's life, by appointing his twin sons as guiding stars in the heavens.

## POOR LEO PARENT EXAMPLE
Akrisos, who banished his daughter, Danae, to a tower of bronze; then put her and her baby son into a chest and set them afloat to save his pride.

# Parentus
## Virgonus

24 August – 23 September

THERE IS NOT ENOUGH DARKNESS IN THE WORLD TO EXTINGUISH
THE LIGHT OF A SMALL CANDLE. — Spanish proverb

This hardworking but sensitive, sometimes self-doubting, star of the Zodiac has the ability to make it up there with the greats where parenting is concerned. However, the Sign of Virgo is far more complex than most people credit, and it is highly important this inborn intricacy be in a state of harmonious synthesis, not a tangle of loose ends, for successful parenting. Why? Because your Virgoan's otherwise splendid ability with children could short-circuit, possibly producing little behavioral peculiarities and nervous anxiety.

The Virgo star with a good childhood behind them usually has no problem in becoming a parent, as they have seen how it's done. (And it's pertinent to remember how the more ancient astrological depictions had the Virgin with an ear of corn in one hand and a child on her lap, symbolizing fertility and the work necessary to produce it.) We must also remember that the "Virgin" represents the pure and unspoiled, and is present in the Virgo star as a desire for purity and perfection — which can get rather mangled if little Virgo is made to feel awkward and unworthy. So, Virgoans with poor role models, or who have been badly misunderstood through the growing up process should not rush into parenthood until they feel the appropriate sense of equipoise has been reached within. (Virgoans are quite psychic in their own particular way. The balanced Virgo star sources quite a lot of information through this.) The Virgoan's partner can be of tremendous help here. Just give your star unqualified love and approval, let them know they are very much your special one, to set rapid inner healing and positive realignment into action. (The health principle flows strongly through this Sign, and when not impeded by impressions laid down by old hurts and painful memories, can work miracles.) Be sure to be careful your Virgo doesn't agree to having a child simply because they want to please you. Virgoans have a strong desire to serve, which is why they are amongst the finest beings on the planet, but they need to be clear on their motives.

With all the above having been spelled out, it can now safely be said that the Virgoan star who is happy with who they are, and who they are with, makes an exceptional parent. Virgo's infant will be the tidiest, cleanest and most spruce little baby bundle around. From the time of conception (possibly before!) the Virgoan parent-to-be most likely read up and studied all facets of parenthood, right down to browsing through name lists in search of appropriate possibilities. Quite some attention will be devoted to the details of infant nutrition as well. Some Virgoan parents in waiting will take up knitting needles or hammer and nails to make essentials for the expected babe with their own crafty hands. Attention should be given to maintaining the calm and composure of the Virgo star, avoiding stress and resting that busy central nervous system through the gestation process. Light, but frequent and wholesome food intake is also recommended for the sensitive Virgoan digestive system at this time. With a nourished nervous system and healthy inner functioning, your Virgo star will simply sail through the, sometimes arduous, early days of parenting, showing the wonderful and resourceful mettle they are made of.

Baby's arrival into the world will be surrounded by great joy. Newborn infant and Virgo parent will quizzically behold each other, and then fall in deep love forever. Reliable routine will accompany the lucky child's top-notch care. Food labels will be critically scanned so that only those with natural ingredients will make it through the door. Even little babe's bedding and clothing is likely to be all natural fibers. This kind of thought will also apply to schooling, the well-adjusted Virgoan parent seeking the type of learning situation which naturally encourages the child's development.

PROGENY'S ADDENDUM: Your in-tune Virgoan star parent is not only efficient and devoted, they also bring a lot of fun into your life. There is always something subtly different and original about the Virgo parent — and when positively launched, that makes for a uniquely delightful individual. This becomes the source of many precious and wonderful memories for the child of such a Virgo. You'll know from their own baby picture placed next to your crib, the poems and pictures just for you, the excursions to edifying edifices and super outdoor picnics, plus pets and ball games, all accompanied by your Virgo parent's sage (and sometimes very comical!) comments, that you are treasured in your star parent's universe and hold a special place in their heart.

Remember how you'd take your questions to your Virgo parent and always get answers, even if not the ones you expected? (The enigmatic nature of Virgo can always come up with surprises.) You loved the way they explained the miracles of nature and creatures to you, and adored the clever stories they could quickly make up. You know that these, along with many other priceless memories of your sometimes extraordinary progenitor, contribute to make you the successful adult you are today. And continue to do so. Even now, you can hardly wait to gather around the family hearth for updates on the latest project. Whether dealing with the family tartan or family politics, you know your star parent will have it figured out in their unique style. Another inspiring mystery of your Virgoan star parent is how can someone so seemingly conventional be so charmingly unconventional underneath?!

## POSITIVE VIRGOAN KEYWORDS
Considerate * Trustworthy * Original

## NOT SO POSITIVE VIRGOAN KEYWORDS
Aloof * Negative * Finicky

## GOOD VIRGOAN PARENT EXAMPLE

Apollo, who endowed his son, Aesculapius, with such skill in the healing art that he could restore life to those on their death bed.

## POOR VIRGOAN PARENT EXAMPLE

Daedalus, who fashioned wings for himself and his son, Icarus, in order to escape to Sicily; but due to incomplete advice from his father, Icarus fell into the sea and drowned.

# Parentus
## Librus

24 September – 23 October

DECISION IS ONE OF THE DUTIES OF STRENGTH. — H. G. Wells

Where does the Libran star rate on the scale of parenting power? Why, right at the top end, of course. As most of us know, this star of the Zodiac feels right at home in the realm of the top-notch. (Platinum bathroom fittings, eclectic ancient Egyptian furniture and luxurious bedrooms, all arrayed with impeccable style and décor are the kind of things that pop into mind when thinking of a Libran home, for example.) But how many of us know that luxury-loving Libra will also work hard and strive determinedly to get there? Although this star may move with caution, they progress steadily toward their goals. Because of knowing how to employ subtle techniques to get what they want, one may be forgiven for not seeing the mighty motivation that drives many Librans. The "lazy Libra" label is often used to mask the powerful ambition at work behind the scenes. The Libran exquisite intuition, diplomacy and pleasing personality are also employed in smoothing the way to success.

All of this is brought to the parenting role. Thus it is not hard to see how the Libran parent can produce a well-adjusted child, segueing into a successful adult. From employing the charm that secures their child the only place left at the best of schools, to endowing their offspring with the social skills and fine manners that will always unlock the doors to success, the Libran parent has got it covered.

But we are way ahead of ourselves here. Libra does like to weigh the pros and cons. With something as life-shaping (in more ways than one) as the decision to have a child, Libra is likely to take even longer than most to deliberate upon the issue. (However, not always. Loving Libra, in the juicy days of early adulthood, may be with child without even thinking about it!) This time, of course, must be given to them. But, be warned, once a yes decision is made, all is likely to move fairly quickly. (If it's vice-versa and the Libran's set to go, awaiting on the partner's decision, it's likely you'll find yourself seduced into action before you know it — when the Libran star is clear on what they want, they know how to get it!) Conception, foremost obstetrician, deluxe nursery decorating, best baby linen, best baby everything really, will follow in rapid-fire time, if not necessarily in that order.

Being an air Sign, Libra is highly mental and intellectual. This mental agility may not be easily apparent, covered as it can be by an easy, relaxed, friendly appearance. (Mind you, if pushed beyond even-tempered and calm, the Libran star can surprise with a sudden and somewhat fierce temper.) But don't be fooled, as this quick wit can translate into unseen worry if your Libran is uneasy for any reason. This is the last thing desired during the gestation process, so do make sure the Libran parent-to-be's mind is at ease now. Good communication and beautiful moments together will be of great help in this effort. Make sure your Libran drinks plenty of spring water to keep the system flushed and functioning well. Ensure they balance work, rest and play in the most efficacious way also. No staying up overnight and painting expected baby's bedroom, for example. That only puts the Libran out of balance and strains the system. Headaches and other problems are the likely result. Watch your Libran at the cookie jar or the chocolate box now too. You may need to suggest that they swap some of these for natural sweets such as fruit, honey or carob.

However, Libra likes to look their best and, usually, do their best. This will translate, on the whole, as a desire to do their best through the pregnancy. The right calcium intake for mother and child's needs will be calculated, along with the correct amount of exercise, not to mention Dior diapers if possible, during this preparation time. Another thing the Libran star wouldn't mind factoring in now for the near future would be a nanny. So helpful for those night shifts! But, where that's not possible, your star will cheerfully see to the little newborn's needs (as long as you do too), as the power of love is a very strong force in the Libran life.

This becomes even more obvious at delivery time. It is like a nimbus of love surrounds the whole procedure, despite the physical discomfort that birth can bring. There's something bigger than Ben Hur going on here, and when the child is put into their Libran parent's arms you can almost see those heavenly choirs you hear singing.

**PROGENY'S ADDENDUM:** Blessings will indeed flow for the tiny newborn — your Libran star parent will see to that. From the early days of an army of friends and associates calling to pay homage and offer congratulations (not to mention great gifts piling at the door!), to godparents of great influence at your christening, to your Libran parent's fortunate connections that helped start your adult career on a successful note, you know you had a pretty charmed childhood. You weren't able to get away with murder (who'd want to anyway?), but you were cut a lot of slack. However, you did know how far you could go before that famous Libran temper came whirling out of the closet, to give everyone a fright. You also knew, deeply and profoundly, the undying force of your star parent's love for you, which you completely reciprocated from day one — and before. And still do. The pride and joy you have brought your Libran parent means a great deal to you. You adore seeing that merry twinkle in their eyes when the parental gaze rests on you, and love the friendship you share as an adult with your Libran parent. You don't mind that most of your friends become friends of said parent — but how come your Libran parent is still bopping when others are dropping, and remains looking gorgeous to boot?! You can thank Venus's enjoyment of and participation in her star child's activities for that. It is hard to outclass a Libran!

## POSITIVE LIBRAN KEYWORDS
Idealistic * Cooperative * Charming

## NOT SO POSITIVE LIBRAN KEYWORDS
Indecisive * Dependent * Self-indulgent

## GOOD LIBRAN PARENT EXAMPLE
Olympias, whose courage and close following of the advice given, brought her son, Alexander the Great, safely into the world to unite it.

## POOR LIBRAN PARENT EXAMPLE
Helios, whose inability to refuse his son Phaethon's request to drive the celestial chariot resulted in Phaethon's death, as he could not control the divine steeds.

# Parentus
## Scorpius
24 October – 22 November

# THE GREATEST GRIEFS ARE THOSE WE CAUSE OURSELVES.
— Sophocles

Can the strong-willed, sometimes loner, instincts of the Scorpio star adapt to parenting? Well, not exactly like a duck takes to water, but pretty close. That is if they have had time to cogitate upon whether they are ready to commit to parenthood, the alterations in lifestyle this will bring, and have come up with a yes decision. The Scorpio who has parenthood thrust upon them may not cope so well. On the surface the Scorpion may appear to but, with this Sign of the Zodiac, still waters run deep, very deep. This powerful and intense star, which likes to be in control of their life, could carry an inner resentment if tricked into the parenting role without any say in the matter. Needless to say this is not good for parent or child, and could cause problems rather than solve any. So do not spring any surprises on your Scorpio star. Instead, make very sure that they have willingly agreed to the miracle of bringing a child into this world to care for.

But when this Sign of the Zodiac has consented to parenting you have fathering or mothering power par excellence! Why? First, this is the Sign to which sex, life and regeneration belong; it is the Zodiac sector that has domain over the mysteries of life, including birth and death. Therefore, the Scorpio who throws their power behind procreating and child rearing is likely to conceive quickly, plus find the pregnancy and birthing process quite fascinating and instructive. This is a strong as well as a "fertile" Sign, and the delivery room should be relatively hassle-free. And second, having chosen to become a parent, the Scorpio star brings a certain kind of wizardry to their child rearing. The insight they have into their child can be extraordinary, and the Scorpion knows exactly what to do and say at any given moment. Furthermore, the deep bond between parent and child is able to be employed to galvanize the offspring through example, inspiration and, most of all, loving, unique, magical humor.

Just to recap: the essential ingredient to successful Scorpio star parenting is their decision to take it on. Having firmly established this core principle, one can now also point out that destiny is always a strong force in the Scorpio life, and this is no different when it comes to having children — in fact, probably more so. Another good reason why the Scorpio star needs to feel the time is right. They know that the triplicity of destiny, fate and kismet enjoy playing in their life and can be met around the corner at any turn, or sneak up on them. But those born under Pluto-ruled Scorpio are more than a match for this set of affairs, and more than a few times rather enjoy meeting with the subtext of existence. However, feeling securely at the helm of their own life is vital to emerging victorious in these encounters. Mind you, it is not always plot and strategy. Many times the instant karma operating is of great good and powerfully enriching. It is very likely you will see the beauty of cosmic design weaving miracles around the agreeable Scorpio parent-to-be.

Nonetheless, do watch over your expectant Scorpio. Most Scorpio stars consider themselves to be "tough," and they are indeed that. (Your average Scorpion can endure situations that would quickly break many others, and end up transforming or annihilating the causes of it. The old adage to beware messing with a Scorpio has a lot of truth in it.) However, this could translate into not taking proper care of themselves through the gestation process. Overworking, not ensuring correct nutrition intake, or that the body is not eliminating wastes regularly — that kind of thing. But by gently and lovingly prompting your Scorpion's awareness of the necessity to healthily nurture the body and mind during this period, they most surely will. (Swimming could be a helpful exercise technique now as well.) As this star likes to be involved in important works, and dislikes trivialities with a vengeance, preferring to be fully engrossed in whatever the task at hand, it won't take much to get them to channel energies in the right direction if they are not already doing so.

This means that events in the delivery suite will not only run wonderfully smoothly, but also be imbued with the hallmarks of powerfully positive destiny. The profound love nature and the deeply loyal, once given, emotions of the Scorpio star will be activated to level one. When the newborn is laid in the arms of their Scorpio parent, the infant feels supremely secure and bathed in love. This superb start to life together becomes further cemented by the Scorpio star's loving attendance on, and shrewd understanding of, the little one in the crucial following weeks.

PROGENY'S ADDENDUM: As you were growing up it was with the awareness that your Scorpio parent is there for you 100 percent. (So much so that you may have learned to be careful in taking hurts and injustices inflicted upon you to your Scorpio progenitor, as they'd set out on immediate and severe retribution. You can still remember the swimming instructor's look of fright when your Scorpio parent loomed at the door!) All questions could be asked of your unshockable and, mostly, unflappable parent, and helpful boundaries would have been set on what was acceptable behavior and what was not.

Your Scorpio parent enthusiastically supported your activities (to the extent of "What?! There's no soccer club?! We'll start one!") and was legendary as a fundraiser. The example set and instruction given you by your Scorpio parent has imbued you with the confidence and courage to go after your all-important goals in adult life. Even now, the depth of love between you is as potent as it ever was. And you know that if ever your back's to the wall, you have a secret weapon — your Scorpio parent!

## POSITIVE SCORPIO KEYWORDS
Courageous * Ambitious * Resourceful

## NOT SO POSITIVE SCORPIO KEYWORDS
Sarcastic * Vindictive * Resentful

## GOOD SCORPIO PARENT EXAMPLE
Metabus, who took with him his daughter Camilla as he fled his city which was torn apart by civil unrest. With enemies in hot pursuit, they reached a flooded river, whereupon Metabus tied his daughter to his spear, called on the gods, and hurled her safely to the other side.

## POOR SCORPIO PARENT EXAMPLE
Cronos, the ruler of the Titans, who, paranoid that one of his offspring would dethrone him, devoured his children — except one who got away, and did eventually topple him.

# Parentus
# Sagittarius

23 November – 22 December

FAITH IS A BIRD THAT FEELS DAWN BREAKING AND SINGS WHILE IT IS STILL DARK. — Old Scandinavian saying

How would this freedom-loving star of the Zodiac adapt to being a parent? With great difficulty, you may be forgiven for thinking. But this isn't necessarily the case, and the key resides in some of the very reasons one may consider free-wheeling Sagittarius unlikely parent material. As well as that instinctive dislike of being fenced in on anybody else's terms but their own, more than a few Sagittarians can appear to be interested only in matters pertaining to themselves. Regaling friends with the ins and outs of current trials and tribulations, elaborating at great length and so forth, only to give short shrift to a friend seeking a sympathetic ear can be typical. "Well, you should have been more careful," is the likely response. "I'll have to go now, I'm packing," or "The cat's on fire" — anything to bump said friend off the line will follow only foolish (and useless!) persistence. (Mind you, strike the Archer at the right time and they'll not only listen, but also give very sage advice.)

Sports, personal, professional and love life, as well as the latest project, spring to mind as topics this colorful Sign of the Zodiac is keen to expound upon. There is no denying that the Sagittarian subjective world is strongly lit by the "me" light. However, this also transposes into causes they choose to identify with. The Sagittarian who identifies with global peace, for example, will actively work to bring this about with indomitable enthusiasm. In other words, the Sagittarius star who sees beyond the bounds of lone ego is able to put that same vital energy and great force into more universal concerns. Highly successfully it must also be said. Generous Jupiter, also known as Zeus, king of the gods, looks after his children well — especially when they are on the right track.

Jovial Jupiter also inclines his star tribe to do things in a big way (with Jupiter being the giant of the planets in our solar system it's no wonder), and do them well. So by now, you should be getting my drift. Once the Sagittarian, after having really thought about it, has decided to become a parent, that lively and resourceful inner world clicks into place behind this decision and nothing will be spared in making it become a successful reality. This is a clever, as well as a questing Sign, so your Sagittarian will have fully understood that a certain level of curtailment comes with early parenting (however, it is not uncommon to see a Sagittarius parent jetting off with young infant to backpack around Greece or hike the Swiss Alps), but will be eager to use this time creatively. Singing songs to baby, making funny faces, doing a little jig around the room — that kind of thing.

But we are getting ahead of ourselves here. Once conception has taken place, your Sagittarian will plough most enthusiastically into the marvels of the pregnancy process, and into getting the world into shape for baby's arrival. You may also be surprised to see a highly sensible side to your Sagittarian surface too. This person, who loves to party, is now talking sensible diet and the wisdom in good sleep patterns. However, if they are not, you should step in and assist your star in stepping back from excessive behavior. Just reminding them that the little one in the making depends on the Sagittarian star factoring their welfare in during the gestation period should do it. Waking up to the trust now placed in them will further inspire the Sagittarian parent-to-be. Also make sure your Sagittarian gets enough rest and doesn't rush about and get frazzled. Resting with a good book on baby matters, with legs elevated, is a good practice at least once daily. The Sagittarian nervous system can tie itself up in knots, so chill out and relax time also allows calm to sort things out here.

Sagittarians are usually a pretty healthy lot (that is if over indulgence isn't taking its toll!), and that's why you see them well represented on the sports field, as well as able to coast through the birthing procedure quite naturally and complication-free. There could even be a cheer in the delivery suite as the newborn makes an entrance. Certainly warm, friendly love will welcome the little one's arrival. Their Sagittarian parent will eagerly, but gently, clasp the new baby to their bosom, after scanning the tiny face to see the blood ties — hints of Papa's nose and Mama's forehead will be joyfully announced. After squads of visitors come to view the Sagittarian star parent's offspring, the infant will be taken home to an abode filled with bonhomie and plenty of stimulation. Baby will be fed, bathed and bedded as any little infant should but, from the start, will be treated as an equal. Someone in a little body waiting to grow up, but providing lots of fun and laughs with first smiles, burps and other early developments, as the Sagittarian gets on with the parenting. Little babe will get lots of enthusiastic encouragement and, with sparkling eyes, really enjoy being spoken to as a peer — that is when the parent is not hamming it up in such a manner as to bring chortles of delight from their little one. Anecdotal evidence has it that children of Sagittarians are the first to laugh. They are amongst the first to walk and talk too, as they really want to keep up with their beloved and energetic parent. That usually sees them in a sports team before kindergarten, and with a well travelled passport before school age.

**PROGENY'S ADDENDUM:** The good fortune, fun and friends that follow your Sagittarian parent permeated your early days with an optimism that has never left you. Indeed, you've inherited a little of their star-spangled good luck, and that, as well as a good education, has led you to great success today. You and your star parent are great buddies, but you absolutely respect them too. You know you can turn to them if you need advice in a tight corner, and you have loads of fun when out together. But why is it the moment anyone claps eyes on the pair of you, they always enthusiastically greet your Sagittarian star parent first, and then turn to you? Well, the nimbus of Jupiter is quite potent — and it will always look after you too, so you'll just have to try and get over it.

## POSITIVE SAGITTARIAN KEYWORDS

Honest * Optimistic * Dependable

## NOT SO POSITIVE SAGITTARIAN KEYWORDS

Tactless * Boastful * Dictatorial

## GOOD SAGITTARIAN PARENT EXAMPLE

Hathor, the goddess of love, mirth, and social joy, who brought her daughter Isis up so well that she became ancient Egypt's principal goddess.

## POOR SAGITTARIAN PARENT EXAMPLE

Priam, king of Troy, whose support of his son Paris in the abduction of the already married Helen led to the devastation of the Trojan War.

# Parentus
## Capricornus

23 December – 20 January

IT IS NOT HOW YOU LOOK AT THE WORLD THAT MATTERS, BUT HOW YOU ACT. — Buddha

Does ambitious Capricorn have good odds when it comes to parenting? Taking into account how this star likes to study the angles of any project before committing to it, if they say yes to bringing a child into the world you can be quite sure they are ready for what is entailed. Add to this the Capricornian strong desire to succeed at whatever they do, and the answer has to be in the affirmative.

The natural caution of the Capricorn star, the same needed by the mountain goat as it carefully navigates the narrow and sometimes precipitous path to the top, prevents a headlong rush into the unknown until there has been a chance to survey it all. Decisions are never made rapidly. Do not spring any surprises or try to ambush your Capricorn into the parenting situation. The weight of the world can sometimes seem heavy enough on this star's shoulders, and loading them up with more unasked for responsibility can produce negative consequences. (What happens when the last straw is laid on the camel's back comes to mind.) So don't endanger your Capricorn's peace of mind through subversive tactics or ultimatums; rather, openly discuss the prospect of parenting. That way you will be sure the wonderful qualities your Capricorn star has to bring to the task of child rearing will transfer intact.

You will also have lassoed the legendary power of the Capricornian force of ambition. Once a little one is agreed upon, endeavor will not stop until that outcome is reached. This patient, hardworking Sign of the Zodiac is famous for the ability to steadfastly pursue significant goals. Their self-discipline and capacity to delay gratification enables achievement of long-lasting success. The "conservative" and "traditional" aspects to the Capricorn make-up ensure the child comes into a world ready to do all the right things by it, courtesy of their Capricorn star parent.

Fruitless worry and pessimistic thinking are to be ruled out of the Capricorn's world during the gestation period. Giving your Capricorn much praise and lots of encouragement will greatly help here; as will showing your honest love and affection for them. (Serious Saturn, provider of the distinctive backbone which distinguishes so many great Capricorn achievements, can also sometimes push buttons of "insecurity" and "inferiority" if there's not much emotional warmth around.) Healthy sources of extra vitamin C and calcium are also a good idea now, along with sensible eating and regular bone strengthening exercise. (Beetroot, barley and spinach are food the Capricorn system can uniquely benefit from.) Attention to dental hygiene would not go amiss either. Camomile tea is soothing for the Capricorn star, and they should stay warm and out of draughts.

"Quality" and "appearance" are words important to this Zodiacal star. Some people interpret this as "snobbery." This is not strictly true.

Capricorns appreciate things that last. Quality goods usually do. Therefore, where possible, the Capricorn will choose a top range Mercedes over a mass-produced model, for example. (Although they are shrewd bargainers!) Capricorns also have a soft and feeling heart within. One way to protect this is to look as good as possible, plus have some kind of status — whether that be top of their profession, politics or the best house in the street. True, the Capricorn star can sometimes use these criteria as a shorthand method of weeding out who they will associate with. (Those selected as friends will find themselves blessed with unswerving loyalty.) Once in a committed relationship, the Capricorn is loath to leave it, as they believe in law and order and respect tradition. That includes the family. This all translates into the world of the Capricorn parent-to-be as sourcing top quality for the price, prenatal and delivery care, along with the best, cost-effective, nursery gear and accoutrements. (It's ditto for all schooling.) Your Capricorn will take all that's happening seriously, and there will be no catching them ill-prepared or early. In fact, this is one of the Signs most likely to have the suitcase packed, under the bed and ready to go before many other Signs would have bought the first matinee set!

Dependable Capricorn is great in any kind of crisis. This star's sound practical advice helps many get their lives back on track. These traits combine in the delivery suite to minimize hassles and maximize childbirth proceeding according to plan. When the precious moment arrives and the newborn is in the Capricorn parent's arms, both feel enormous love. It seems like fate has decreed this moment. The bonding is instant and permanent. The christening gown may already await at home, and it is likely that it has come down through the family. Certainly the little one experiences this quality in the warmth of their Capricorn parent's love as well — a most reassuring feeling of "place."

Once home, this star parent will have all highly organized to attend to the infant. Baby will be fed, bathed and burped on schedule. Even better if the services of a nanny can be employed. But no matter if not — industrious Capricorn will take it all in their stride. However, as the child grows, this star parent may need to remember to lighten up a little. Fun is a necessary part of growing up, but some Capricorn parents have little time for trivia and bury themselves in work or something, resulting in kids feeling shut out. Capricorn's disciplinarian side, along with high expectations of said kids, can be a little daunting if an effort's not made to correct it.

**PROGENY'S ADDENDUM:** But not *your* Capricorn star parent! All along, you've seen beyond that aloof face presented to the world and cuddled into the warm heart within. Great understanding exists between you and your star parent, and many times you've quietly comforted them in times of gloom, disappointment in the world or whatever. But the good times you've had together far outnumber these moments — like when your wily Capricorn parent's ways have secured a unique situation for the family: sitting at the captain's table while cruising, or being personally invited to Disneyland, for example. Throughout your childhood, you felt your star parent's love for you, solid as a mountain, and have been privy to their funny ways. That wry Capricorn humor has completely cracked you up — when you've understood it! Even now, the paradox that is your parent stimulates you to make the best of yourself. But why is it they have hardly aged a nanosecond in years?! That's another of Saturn's mysteries.

## POSITIVE CAPRICORN KEYWORDS
Efficient * Patient * Charismatic

## NOT SO POSITIVE CAPRICORN KEYWORDS
Suspicious * Worry * Self-doubting

## GOOD CAPRICORN PARENT EXAMPLE
Sir Pellinore, whose excellent instruction of his son, Sir Percival, enabled him to be the only Knight of the Round Table to win sight of the Holy Grail.

## POOR CAPRICORN PARENT EXAMPLE
King Gordius, whose failure to instill balanced values in his son Midas resulted in Midas choosing over all wishes that everything he touched would turn to gold — not taking into account that this also meant food and loved ones.

# Parentus

## Aquarius

21 January – 19 February

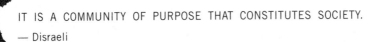

IT IS A COMMUNITY OF PURPOSE THAT CONSTITUTES SOCIETY.
— Disraeli

**W**ill cool, astute and universal Aquarius gravitate to and function well in the parenting role? Perhaps it's difficult to imagine these collected star people perspiring over infant food formula preparation or pushing the perambulator, but when their heart is truly called, they will. Mind you, it will be done in their unique and original style and, most of the time, competent Aquarius makes it appear effortless.

However, the Aquarian heart stirred with genuine desire to bring a child into this world is the key ingredient. This Zodiac star will not become a parent for mawkish reasons such as may seduce some other Signs. "Oh, my cousin's having a baby, why don't we have one too?!" is very unlikely to be spoken by an Aquarian. And don't try to corral your Aquarian into the parenting ring by appealing to sentiment. That can work as a sure-fire push in the opposite direction. Airing your feelings honestly and being open to discussion is the much better route to take. This is an intelligent Sign, and emotional hyperbole does not fool the Aquarian star. They know having a child is a serious commitment, plus circumscribes a certain amount of personal freedom. Marching to the beat of a different drum as they do, the Aquarian who voluntarily decides on becoming a parent usually makes a much better one as then an undercurrent of rebellion against the constraints on their life isn't there to sabotage parental efforts. Rather it is "au contraire," as these restrictions are welcomed as blocks to build their parental mettle upon. One can set one's clock by the time some Aquarian parents deliver their children to school, for example. And if there's a school fete, they will cheerfully man a white elephant or cake stall, or anything really to help raise funds. Something often overlooked in understanding the Aquarian star is that they take their responsibilities seriously. The much vaunted rampant revolutionary side to Aquarius is what manifests when too many restrictions are placed upon them by society and others. But when these star people elect their own obligations and accountability, expect these to be filled "par excellence."

Another thing close to the Aquarian heart is truth. (It may be their novel take on it, but it will be the truth.) Many Aquarians have inbuilt radar that detects insincerity. But don't think these broad-minded people go around on witch-hunts. They believe in live and let live but won't get involved in what is, to them, patently hypocritical and time wasting. The Aquarius star knows that we are all here for a purpose and is tolerant if you haven't found yours yet, but don't try and stop them living theirs.

All the above illustrates the importance of this star entering the parental role of their own volition. They can then rank amongst the best. Aquarius is a youthful, democratic and liberal Sign, and these qualities work as great staging points for successful parenting. The Aquarian parent can stay apace with offspring's development physically and psychologically, and is also able to work or talk things through to solutions that accommodate all. The innate and acquired wisdom of this star blends well with these traits. Thanks to an inborn alignment with creation's bigger picture, Aquarians also have rather uncanny ESP. When this is working well it informs them of a great deal. It is very difficult to pull the wool over this star's eyes — as many Aquarians' progeny have discovered. And don't think Aquarians are lax in the disciplinarian department. They are highly aware life needs both structure and freedom to evolve to true potential. When the law needs laying down Aquarius can do this consummately — via an intelligent, airy, but emphatic way that is close to genius.

The Aquarian who chooses to become a parent knows they are involved with a cosmic project, and magical synchronicity usually lights the way from the start. But ensure your Aquarian pays proper attention to their physical well-being through the gestation process. They might take enough calcium to give baby strong bones and teeth, but short-change themselves through insufficient diet, exercise or rest. Gentle exercise daily to get the circulation moving is important, as is resting with legs elevated. Yoga and meditation are invaluable for nourishing and relaxing the nervous system. Herbal teas, fresh food and clean air are all tonics for the Aquarian system.

If it seems at the time of birth that the whole universe is present and involved, that's because it is! The Aquarian's cosmic spirit is in contact and the joyous event of the arrival of this star's sacred little trust sets those cosmological bells ringing. A current of high-voltage love ignites as the newborn is placed in their star parent's arms, setting the seal on the purposeful universal design that has brought them together. Both feel deep happiness, a "knowing" this was meant to be, and the world will be made a better place because of it.

**PROGENY'S ADDENDUM:** The strong rapport between you and your Aquarian parent continues throughout childhood. Often your parent seemed to anticipate your needs, and you never had a problem being taken into situations others may have found unorthodox — a channelled teaching session or world peace march, for instance. Being the child of an Aquarian has great rewards. You're treated as a peer, even when little, with fascinating conversations accompanying diaper changes and feeding times. Independence may have been learnt young, but you always knew the safety net of your resourceful Aquarian parent was behind you. Home was stimulating and, despite an assortment of odd bods satelliting the place, you were never left out. Plus your friends were always welcome. The broad outlook you were raised with contributes greatly to the successful person you have become.

The bond forged at birth has become even stronger as your unique destiny together has unfolded. Your love and respect for your star parent is still evident today, as you both get on with individual (highly individual!) projects, but adore gabbing about everything. You can relate to Aquarius's reputation as the "best friend" of the Zodiac (they are very popular people) and whenever you reach out, your amazing Aquarian parent is there to help. The missions your parent becomes involved in range from delightful to awesome. But why, you sometimes ponder, have these multiplied not lessened through time? Where does this phenomenal ability to beneficially affect people come from, and how is it they can still read your mind? Easy — it is the Age of Aquarius, after all!

## POSITIVE AQUARIAN KEYWORDS
Perceptive * Tolerant * Charitable

## NOT SO POSITIVE AQUARIAN KEYWORDS
Eccentric * Thoughtless * Rebellious

## GOOD AQUARIAN PARENT EXAMPLE
Ptah-Hotep, Egyptian god, whose advice to his son for successful and righteous living was studied by children in ancient Egypt for centuries as the "Instruction."

## POOR AQUARIAN PARENT EXAMPLE
Poseidon, whose failure to cultivate in his son, Atlas, compassion and respect for others resulted in Atlas losing his kingdom of Atlantis and being condemned to eternally bear the world on his shoulders.

# Parentus

## Pisceus

20 February – 20 March

TRUST, BUT VERIFY. — Russian proverb

The Pisces star is caring, sensitive and somewhat imaginative; definitely qualities required for successful parenting. However, this deep water Sign can become foggy and disturbed when emotionally hurt and confused. Therefore, it is of utmost importance to be doubly — no, triply! — sure they feel truly ready to become a parent and have clear ideas about what is entailed.

Otherwise the strict reality of being on call twenty-four hours a day could overwhelm romantic and utopian Pisces, and their impressionable nervous system will suffer. Furthermore, because this star desires to please, and can respond to the moment with joyous expressions (it's the opposite when the delicate and sometimes fragile constitution of this Sign is beset by harsh realities), you'd better be certain when they agree to parenting that they still feel that way in the next five minutes, or the following day. There's a smidgen of "martyrdom" in this star, and if you're not observant they might be saying yes when they'd rather be saying no. Obviously, no one benefits in this situation and some quite emotional pain can result when the Piscean is prematurely pushed into parenting.

But the Piscean who is realistically ready to bring a baby into the world makes a very fine parent. As this is one of the "fertile" Signs, it shouldn't take too long before a child is on the way either!

Despite giving the impression that such things do not really concern them, security is important to the Pisces star, especially in a situation involving children. A secure domicile, along with adequate income, are necessary to buttress the Piscean against inner and silent worry, which only erodes their inborn strengths and can also erupt in what appears to others as rather strange behavior. The assurance of love is also needed, so feelings should be expressed lovingly and often. When these conditions are met, the Piscean star thrives. Their faith can move mountains (and does), and the Piscean glows with invincible inner strength and almost mystical luminosity. The balanced Piscean is amazingly photogenic and highly charismatic.

This sympathetic (Pisceans feel for the plight of others, and many desire to help humankind in some way to feel fulfilled) and outwardly gentle Sign (having an inborn reluctance to inflict hurt, and abhorring confrontations) can be prone to fluctuating moods and emotions. The Pisces star can also be highly secretive. This combination means that without warning, like the fury of the sudden sea storms Poseidon–Neptune was famous for, the Pisces will send the greatest tsunami onto your shore, and is already whipping up a dozen more. It's your fault. You were fooled by their acting. (This Sign produces many stars of stage and screen.) You were expected to see past the valiant show being exhibited, come to the rescue and be there.

Keeping a discerning eye on your Pisces makes a great difference. A few kind words or simple suggestions at the right time will work wonders. Pisceans are born romantics. Flowers and candle-lit dinners provided by your thoughtful self, plus a nice gift or two, will quell any developing subterranean tempests, and also demonstrate your love for them. Your Piscean will be strengthened by the power of your love and perception, and the astonishing Piscean ability to manage mighty miracles will be in tip-top shape.

Thus, the well-loved and fully appreciated Piscean brings a fountain of strength and intuitive wisdom to the parenting role. This star's attunement to the mystical love which is at the core of creation, the haze around each and every atom's nucleus within which protons and electrons weave the dance of life, enables access to a supreme order of parenting. Piscean parents have raised many noble spirits who have brought peace and light to our planet. It is said the Buddha's mother was one.

Don't be surprised if angelic forces seem to be around from conception to birth. You may even hear the sound of big golden wings rustling the air — perhaps find the odd feather! Peace of mind is crucial now, and your loving ways help maintain that. Your Pisces may need time alone sometimes to recharge batteries and commune with the developing babe, so respect this. Gentle yoga, swimming and meditation are excellent for the Piscean system, as is a diet rich in seafood, plus plenty of fresh fruit and vegetables. (No junk food!) Bilberries are invaluable for keeping those dreamy Piscean eyes sparkling, and on 20/20 vision.

A calm, content, positively minded Piscean excels in the delivery suite, especially if prenatal classes have been attended. Majestic love surrounds the event, and when the babe is born it will seem even the stars in the firmament register this moment. When the newborn is cradled in their Pisces parent's arms it is like they have known each other forever; two angels from heaven now together on Earth. With a sigh, both will relax in the divine joy between them, and around them.

Devotedly this Zodiac star will attend to the little one's needs from day one, and the child finds great calm in the Pisces parent's presence. A good education, one including the arts and good moral principles as well as the school syllabus, is deemed essential. Employing discipline can be difficult for this parent, but on understanding that over-permissiveness can be detrimental to the child's future prospects, this state of affairs is corrected pretty quickly.

**PROGENY'S ADDENDUM:** As the child of a stable Pisces star, you will always feel protected by your parent's love. Memories of home life brim with warm happiness, underpinned by your Pisces parent's unlimited ability to engender magical moments. (Others aren't immune to Pisces' spell-power either. When the authorities wanted to replace your school with a highway, your amazing parent arranged a meeting and came away with not only the school saved, but more funds allocated!) All the kids clamored to come to your birthday parties — and then had so much fun, they didn't want to leave! Come to think of it, you didn't really want to leave home either! Even now, home and family business is a strong magnet. You love the humor, happiness and successful brainstorming sessions when you're all together. Your Pisces parent is as magical as ever — but you do wonder why everyone you meet always asks after or wants to know more about your star begetter. Really! But you should be used to the mystical fascination your parent kindles in others by now, and accord your Neptunian progenitor the respect everyone else does.

## POSITIVE PISCEAN KEYWORDS
Responsive * Inspiring * Spiritual

## NOT SO POSITIVE PISCEAN KEYWORDS
Hypersensitive * Escapist * Fearful

## GOOD PISCES PARENT EXAMPLE
Margawse of Lothian, who reared her son, Gawain, to be so chivalrous that he became renowned throughout the land and King Arthur's favored knight.

## POOR PISCES PARENT EXAMPLE
Perseis, whose failure to instil wisdom as well as magic in her daughter Circe resulted in the princess casting spells on unfortunate sailors to change them into various animals.

# Attitudes

* ★ If a child lives with criticism, he or she learns to condemn.
* ★ If a child lives with hostility, he or she learns to fight.
* ★ If a child lives with ridicule, he or she learns to be shy.
* ★ If a child lives with shame, he or she learns to feel guilty.
* ★ If a child lives with tolerance, he or she learns to be patient.
* ★ If a child lives with encouragement, he or she learns confidence.
* ★ If a child lives with praise, he or she learns to appreciate.
* ★ If a child lives with fairness, he or she learns justice.
* ★ If a child lives with security, he or she learns to have faith.
* ★ If a child lives with approval, he or she learns self-esteem.
* ★ If a child lives with acceptance, he or she learns to find love in the world.